Song of the Universe

Song of the Universe

Earth Poems and Prose From Around the World

Compiled and Edited

By

Anne Rowthorn

KenArnoldBooks, LLC
Portland, Oregon

Half the profits from the sale of this book are being donated to the Connecticut Chapter of The Nature Conservancy to further their important work. Founded in 1951, The Nature Conservancy states that its mission is to preserve the plants, animals and natural communities that represent the diversity of life on Earth by protecting lands and waters they need to survive.

See pages 235-245 for permissions and copyright notices for individual contributions.

Published by KenArnoldBooks, LLC.
1330 SW 3rd Avenue, #810,
Portland, Oregon 97201
www.kenarnoldbooks.com

Printed in the United States of America.

ISBN: 978-0-9799634-8-3

Library of Congress Control Number: 2008939153

To lovers of the world, these mountains are not a hundred miles away. Their spiritual power and the goodness of the sky make them as near, as a circle of friends. Plain, sky, mountains—you bathe in these spirit-beams, turning round and round, as if warming at a campfire. Presently you loose consciousness of your separate existence. You blend with the landscape, and become part and parcel of nature.

—John Muir,
A Thousand-Mile Walk to the Gulf

To Jeffery,

Forever the song in my life.

Contents

Foreword, by Lee W. Bailey i
Introduction vii

1. The Creation of the Universe 1
2. Earth, Our Mother 23
3. Awe and Adoration 39
4. The Web of Life 57
5. The Solace of Nature 73
6. Air, Sky, and Stars 87
7. The Sun Descends into Night 101
8. The Rhythm of the Seasons 113
9. Forests and Mountains 139
10. The Waters of Life 153
11. Creatures Great and Small 167
12. The Song of the Universe 177
13. Beauty in a Moment 185
14. Remembrance, Regret, and Requiem 195
15. The Dream of the Earth 217

Acknowledgments 233
Permissions and Copyright Notices 235

Foreword

This collection of celebrations of the sacred in nature by Anne Rowthorn is a continuation of an important theme in her other books, such as *Caring for Creation*. How can religion contribute to the analysis of the ecological crisis, she asks, and how can we re-awaken a sense of the sacred in nature in a post-industrial world? The present book is a stimulating, rich exploration of the second theme. It moves the heart toward feeling the presence of the Great Mystery present in nature, and brings up several important issues in the discussion of the role and nature of sacredness in the world. For when we re-awaken the dormant reverence for nature's wonders, we can change our consciousness and restrain the ravaging beast of industrial society's attack on nature, from dynamite-blasting mountaintops for coal to factory fishing ships sucking up the ocean's fish.

A man went into a restaurant, the story goes, skeptical about this organic food thing, but willing to try it. The waitress, a college student in a baggy dress, served his choice of soup in a hand-made ceramic bowl. "Wait," he said, "There is a piece of dirt in this soup." "That's not dirt," she replied, not missing a beat. "That's Mother Earth." Re-awakening the gentle touch of awareness of sacredness in nature is a delicate task, a re-framing of basic metaphysical concepts, so poetic language suits its subtle feel and affects its thinking. A child writes: "In me reside the stars." Another whispers: "The sea talks to me." The deep mystery sought is sometimes wordless, and sometimes peeks through a paradox like: "Be the river." New sensibilities awaken, such as intimacy with the soil, jaw-dropping wonder at the vastness of our view of the stars. New theologies are emerging, re-framing our language and images of sacredness, such as Mother Earth and Goddess Tree, evoked by wise waitresses and Julia Butterfly, who sat high in a tree for two years to stop loggers from cutting it down. She saved the tree.

This book wisely embraces many cultures' voices, many eras' visions of sacredness in nature—Native Americans, Australian Aborigines, Māoris, ancient Chinese sages, Buddhist monks, Hebrew storytellers and prophets, contemporary thinkers and activists, all writers who feel the sacred in their bones and in the waterfalls.

In this book we hear the further emergence of not only a new intimacy, but a new morality of nature. Whereas industrial society stripped nature of inherent value so it could be dominated and exploited, the unanticipated results have led to a "tipping point" where not only global warming threatens, but morality is beginning to be extended beyond human society to nature. Buddhist monks in Asia ordain trees, wrapped with ropes, to stop logging. The growing popularity of organic and vegetarian food expresses heightened moral concerns for chemical pollution and abuse of animals for food. Now more people ask, following Jane Goodall's intimacy with chimpanzees, "do animals have feelings?" Writers in this book press further, asking: "Do insentient beings have feelings?" This question is blatantly absurd to those caught in industrial society's subject/object metaphysic. An experience of sacredness in the world requires a different sensitivity, but a common one. It is present in feeling the wonder of the star-filled sky, awe at the powerful stillness of the rising sun as the earth rotates into its light, or amazement at watching a litter of puppies being born. Sacredness is present in these phenomena.

The holy is emerging, seeming to be magical, eternal, and awesome, from what has too long been portrayed metaphysically as dead matter and senseless animals with no inherent value, for us to dominate for our own pleasure. In this book you are pointed to the eternal in trees, the everlasting in flowers, the living waters. "The love of God is in the very nature of things. . . . [T]he heavens declare the glory of God." Here nature is no longer a ruthless, mathematical working out of iron laws. For our metaphysical picture of the vast cosmos can no longer remain the indifferent machine promoted by industrialists happy to trash it for consumerist pleasure and power. Albert Einstein speaks in this book of our old delusion of separation from nature. Astronauts such as Edgar Mitchell are returning from space journeys with an astonishing reversal: a reverence for the sacred wonders they saw on their journeys seeking the meaning of it all. He left earth as an engineer trained to dominate, but returned bringing clouds of infinite wonder, proclaiming that we are one with the universe.

Invisible bonds hold us all together in this wondrous cosmos, on a blessed planet with just the right conditions for life as we know it. This gift is an amazing gift, compared to the numbers of planets we are discovering with horribly cold, hot, or toxic environments hostile to life. These discoveries, thanks to space science and technology, awaken a new thankfulness for the graceful gifts we share on this planet. We are part of this system. We do not stand outside it and look at it, despite the scientific method that uses that attitude as a useful research tool. Rather we are ultimately highly dependent parts of a tightly linked system. We are now finding that system on our planet disturbed by global warming. The solution to this danger has to include the re-awakening of reverence, of the vitality of sacredness, a new ethic of living with respect for the interlinked wholeness of our world's system that we share. In the face of more storms flooding coastlines, we are called to awaken new spiritual motives higher than consumerist self-indulgence.

Who calls me? sings the poet. What silent song of the universe awakens me from my complacent sleep? What holy wind brings me new sensitivity to the beauty and wonder of life itself on this precious planet? Who calls me to hear the presence of Being, existence itself, in the endless wonders all around us? What power calls me to attend to the silent awe as I behold the spectacle of each night's cosmic display of distant fireballs? God? Goddess? Holy Spirit? Allah? Tao? Buddhamind,? Wakan Tanka? The names are many and the reality is a great mystery hidden in the depths of many such names. The poetic expression of this depth, the silent awe at its vastness, is only brushed by language that points beyond. "When I point to the moon," says the Zen master, "I don't look at my finger; I look at the moon." Don't be trapped in language. Look where it points. Not just "within," where you may feel and think it—not just in a book, no matter how holy—but also "without," where its presence surges both in your own heartbeat and amid the sparkling stars.

The task of poetic awakening to the presence of sacred whispers in nature is challenging enough and exciting enough. We must increase our sensitivities. But there are many issues raised that also require rigorous thinking and discussion. As we take daring steps toward a new culture beyond traditional theology that over centuries wrestled with how to understand and apply sacredness, we must prayerfully rethink some basic positions of traditional religious thought. Dominion is one such theme.

Historically, when technology was weak and global population small, the theological decision to proclaim human dominion over nature, as in the biblical book of Genesis, had a good reason. For millennia, cold, hungry people had feared the world's fierce animals, harsh weather, and health problems such as difficult childbirths. Archaic religion attempted to placate what it saw as angry spirits behind these problems with sacrifices, even blood sacrifices of cherished children, as the Genesis story of Abraham willing to sacrifice his only son Isaac shows. Fear of the spirits was often tied to guilt for sins, personal or collective. This was long practiced worldwide, and in Christianity Jesus is still seen by some as the final sacrifice for believers whose sins are washed away with his blood. So when the ancient Hebrew priests wrote down the creation account in Genesis, they apparently believed that God was telling humans to not fear the spirit world, for He was giving humans dominion over the spirit world and nature to reverse the ancient fear and sacrificial efforts at placation. So the Genesis dominion theology initially had a good purpose. As knowledge and technologies improved the human situation, the psychology of sacrifice out of fear was turned it into a theology of humble self-sacrifice out of law and love. Today commercial-industrial society seeks to limit the notion of sacrifice and promotes self-indulgence instead, which feeds the ecology crisis.

Humans don't need much religious sanction to dominate, since it is an archetypal instinct rooted in the jungle. But when religion sanctions it, the instinct is hard to rein in. So now we must rein it in and put the brakes on the once fruitful but now destructive religious sanction on human domination of nature. We must give up our illusion that humans have the God-blessed right to dominate nature and other people for our own power and pleasure. We must make the radical and huge step away from aggressive domination of nature and shift toward a respectful restraint in our relations to nature, rooted in strong perceptions of the whispers of the sacred in the world.

Another major theological problem is that of suffering. Ancient polytheistic religions explained suffering as battles between various gods. The god of war, such as Mars in Rome, wanted conquest and bravery. The goddess of love, such as Aphrodite in Greece, wanted love and sex. Suffering and victory were seen as the working out of the struggles between the archetypal demands of the gods and goddesses. Homer's *Odyssey* is about a battle between Poseidon, god of the sea, with its raging powers, and Athena, goddess of the city and cultural values of Athens. These powers continue today, perhaps just under the surface of monotheistic religions, in wars, sexual activities, etc., as David Miller pointed out in *The New Polytheism* (1974). Monotheism proclaimed that God is omnipotent, so evil was theoretically conquered. But problems such as Job's suffering of a righteous man lingered. If the divine is ultimately omnipotent, as in the monotheistic religions (Judaism, Christianity, Islam), why are evil and suffering so powerful? The omnipotence of goodness overcoming evil in the big picture certainly makes life hopeful and seeks to overcome despair for believers, but it is sometimes a close race between hope and despair, peace and suffering.

Now if we open new theological horizons to the sacred in nature, how do we explain the powers in nature that do not favor humanity, and have no respect for the either the pious or the aggressive belief in human dominion over nature? Where is the sacred in nature when a shark mangles an innocent girl, when brain cancer takes a precious loved one before their time? Obviously nature is not all sacred in the sense of favoring humans above other parts of the world. Since storms and disease, death and suffering, despair and madness, are part of life on this planet, how do we reconcile the sense of God's love with the pain or evil of such grief? The new theology of the sacred in nature has to answer these questions, and we are just beginning to work on it. Perhaps we will have to relinquish the human pride of elevating our intellect and technological skill that have seemed to make us kings on top. But what does that mean? How then shall we live? Where do we draw the line between protecting our species and honoring the place of others? Shall we relinquish hunting? Some do. Shall we become vegetarian? Some do. Shall we give up keeping animals in cages in zoos? What shall we do when the deer and bears, pushed out of their natural habitat, appear in suburban neighborhoods?

Can we imagine a world without toxic chemicals and nuclear threats? Can we keep our population within the limits that the planet can support? Can we reduce our consumption of energy and resources so we do not choke ourselves on our own pollution and drive up the prices of fuels and other resources? Obviously the effort to do these things has begun in the shadow of the threat of the effects of global warming. But there are baby steps and giant steps. We need to insulate our houses, install compact fluorescent bulbs, recycle much more, drive less and slower, and so forth. But these are baby steps. We also must admit we will have to take giant steps, such as drastically reducing energy use, consumption, pollution, and population. These will be very difficult.

The emerging ecological spirituality that this book evokes is needed to help with these tough cultural shifts. This new spirituality should help motivate the best of our industrial society's skills at inventing new, sustainable technologies. It should help shape new ethics of sustainable living, rather than self-indulgent consumerism. Perhaps it can even refocus our spiritual lives so that we enjoy simpler, slower, less stressful, less acquisitive, more egalitarian and peaceful lives in a world of global cooperation. What new challenges. What giant steps for civilization and religions. Imagine!

—Lee W. Bailey,
Author of *The Enchantments of Technology*,
Department of Philosophy and Religion,
Ithaca College (Retired)

Introduction

Sunday morning had the appearance of a day just waiting for something to happen. It was a postcard-perfect day in the Adirondacks. It was morning and the mist on the moist forest floor was rising under a cloudless sky. The temperature on the late July day was just right, not too hot, not too cool, and all around was the rich fragrance of a thousand balsam trees towering above us. As we slowly rounded the corner of the dirt road we were traveling, a deer suddenly appeared in front of the car and there she stayed. The light from the sun's rays revealed her contours—her sleek, slender legs, her long neck and triangular face with ears that seemed oversized, her flawless tan matt coat, and especially her round black eyes that seemed to look right at us and through us. She was so close we could almost see her eye lashes, but she didn't blink. She just stared. Time froze; then just as suddenly as she appeared, she tilted slightly backwards, raised her front legs, and with a leap bounded up the bank, into the woods, and away. For a moment the three of us in the car were silent. Then the philosopher among us asked the simple question: Is the deer inherently beautiful, or is beauty solely in the eye of the beholder?

We had brought a certain sense of expectation. We were ready to be impressed by the passing deer; this was summer under optimal conditions. Also, we all probably had an expanded and developed sense of vision to see and register the extreme beauty of the deer for, in addition to myself and the philosopher in the car, the other passenger was a poet. But if it was winter in the hunting season, might not another person, especially if he were a hunter carrying a rifle by his side, see the deer and think, "Fine, here is a month of dinners for my freezer." He might perceive the deer as an object for his use, and perhaps we might have been that hunter also, if the circumstances had been different.

There is no substitute for experience. Only by letting the earth speak directly to us, only by being immersed in the natural world—on the vast desert, in the dense, fragrant forest, by the fresh river—will appreciation and affection for the earth be nurtured. But poets and prose writers and philosophers offer us a multitude of ways to see the earth. They open earth's door and invite us to step into the garden of the universe.

The nineteenth-century poet and landscape painter of the Hudson River School, Christopher Pearce Cranch, illustrates the power of just one well-crafted selection of ecological writing. Having graduated from the Harvard Divinity School, he was headed toward ordination in the Unitarian Church and professional life as a New England pastor. Then he inadvertently came upon Ralph Waldo Emerson's essay, "Nature." It changed his life. He never stepped into the pulpit of a church again. The forest became his pulpit, and he spent the rest of his life painting and writing about it.

Harry Thurston, the compiler of *The Sea's Voice*, an anthology of Atlantic Canadian writings, said that, "... nature writing is not only (or even primarily) about the wilderness and what you find in it, but it presents the individual with a way of seeing." From the smallest literary form, the haiku, to the narrative poem and the essay; the writings in this book present the reader with ways of seeing the natural world.

Nature writing at its best invites the reader, through his and her imagination, to become part of the natural world being described. This is why nature writing is so refreshing. Its authenticity speaks to us. When the celebrated American poet, Maya Angelou states that ". . . A river sings a beautiful song—Come rest here by my side" (from "On the Pulse of Morning"), we are right there in our minds beside the poet refreshing ourselves in the clear, pristine river. We get the same impression of being immersed in the landscape by reading a poem of a very different age. Du Xunhe, a poet of T'ang era (ninth century B.C.E) in China wrote:

I sit and watch
The flower-like moon
And the sparkling stars
Fade from the sky.
The shadows of the mountains
And the far reaches of the tides.

There is a lot of room between the artfully crafted words for the reader to fill in the spaces and become part of the evening landscape fading as morning approaches. It is as if we were sitting quietly beside the poet watching "the flower-like moon and the sparkling stars fade from the sky." The same feeling of being a part of the landscape is evoked when the contemporary Czech philosopher, Erazim Kohák, describes the approach of night. "The night comes softly, almost imperceptibly. The darkness gathers unnoted amid the undergrowth, in the shelter of the hemlocks and beneath the boulders of the old dam, slowly seeping out to cover the ground" (*The Embers and the Stars*).

Nature writing evokes an appreciation for the natural world; it widens one's understanding of one's self as a part of—not apart from—it; it awakens in the reader a perception of its beauty and even its sacredness; and finally it arouses a feeling of concern for its well-being and its future. If there is any commonality in the writings presented in this book it is that each selection could be described as having at least one of these attributes.

The deer's appearance crystallized for me the reason I am passionate about collecting beautiful and sometimes challenging and evocative ecological writings and why I compiled this book. Through its variety of selections, I hope that readers will become sensitized to the awe, and even the sacredness of nature, so that when they are suddenly arrested by a deer in front of their car, they will view it with a sense of awe, recognizing a fellow being on this planet that is part of the remarkable web of life we call earth. I would like *The Song of the Universe* to enhance the reader's vision. I hope the eye of the reader will be opened wide to see, to comprehend, to be filled with awe, and then to cherish, guard, and protect nature, perceived in its inherent beauty, unfiltered by the written page.

I

The Creation of the Universe

To stand at the edge of the sea, to sense the ebb and flow of the tides, to feel the breath of a mist moving over a great salt marsh, to watch the flight of shore birds that have swept up and down the surf lines of the continents for untold thousands of years, to see the running of the old eels and the young shad to the sea, is to have knowledge of things that are as nearly eternal as any earthly life can be.

—Rachael Carson,
The Sea Around Us

Well I'll Be

A Filipino Creation Story

Author Unknown

"Well I'll Be," a Filipino creation story, was identified by Matthew Fox when he was leading a creation spirituality workshop in the Philippines. A significant feature of this account is that God, the Great Spirit who created the universe, is portrayed as feminine.

In the beginning the Great Spirit created the Universe. Now the universe was dark. So the Great Spirit said, "Let there be light." And behold, light appeared.Then the Great Spirit said, "Let the heavens be." And behold, the heavens blossomed into galaxies filled with stars, planets and moons.

The Great Spirit said, "Let the plants be." And behold, the Earth began to green with mosses, ferns, vines, trees, flowers and grasses.

Then the Great Spirit said, "Let the animals be." And behold, countless creatures emerged to crawl, walk, fly, and swim over the land, sea and sky.

All creatures needed and helped each other to stay alive. The sun gave its life to the plants; the plants gave their lives to the animals; the animals gave their lives to the worms; the worms gave their lives to the soil; and the soil gave its life to the plants.

The sun's heat formed clouds that watered the rainforest; the forest's canopy caught the lashing rain and dropped it gently into streams and rivers that continually watered the lowlands.

The rivers passed through the mangrove forests bringing water and soil for the trees. The swamp, in turn, purified the muddy rivers for the coastal reefs which need crystal clear water to survive.

Soon all creatures on earth began to sing:

> "This earth spun of soil and sun,
> Water and air for all to share,
> Lives or dies by the work and play
> Of every creature, every day."

The Great Spirit danced to the song of her creation. "Well I'll be!" She exclaimed, "This is wonderful."

The suddenly the first humans appeared, for the Great Spirit had accidentally created creatures in her own image when she said, "Well I'll be." And today, human beings feel most alive when they dance with the song of the earth and sky.

God Paints the Rainbows

Barb Laski

The contemporary poet, Barb Laski, says that the last stanza of her elegant poem on the omnipotence of the creator God of the universe is an adaptation of a Dietrich Bonhoeffer quotation: "The Earth remains our Mother as God is our Father, and only the one who remains true to the Mother will be placed by her in the arms of the Father."

God paints the rainbows,
And hangs the moon and the stars,
Perfumes the flowers with benevolent grace,
Among soft grass of alpine lace.

God pulls at the tides,
And tosses the waves,
Sings hymns with birds aloft in air,
Chasing wind songs in silent prayer.

God spins the earth,
And scatters the clouds,
Makes sunbeams dance,
In a heavenly trance.

God is our Father
And the Earth is our Mother.
Love of our Mother so cherished and kind,
Delivers us to our Father eternally divine.

As You Leave Eden Behind You

Chaim Stern

"As You Leave Eden Behind You," a reflection from a Jewish prayer book, is an invitation to us all to reach back to our archaic roots to the dawn of humanity, to "recollect more deeply. . . . Where the trees deepest roots drink from the abyss." Echoed through this selection is the idea of exile and the call to come home to basic simplicities of being.

Of all created things the source is one,
Simple, single as love; remember
The cell and seed of life, the sphere
That is, of child, white bird, and small blue dragon-fly,
Green fern, and the gold four-petalled tormentilla
The ultimate memory.
Each latent cell puts out a future,
Unfolds its differing complexity
As a tree puts forth leaves, and spins a fate
Fern-traced, bird-feathered, or fish-scaled.
Moss spreads its green film on the moist peat,
The germ of dragon-fly pulses into animation and takes wing
As the water-lily from the mud ascends on its ropy stem
To open a sweet white calyx to the sky.

Humankind has further to travel from simplicity,
From archaic moss, fish, and lily parts,
And into exile travels a long way.

As you leave Eden behind you, remember your home,
For as you remember back into your own being
You will not be alone; the first to greet you
Will be those children playing by the burn,
The otters will swim up to you in the bay,
The wild deer on the moor will run beside you.

Recollect more deeply, and the birds will come,
Fish rise to meet you in their silver shoals,
And darker, stranger, more mysterious lives
Will throng about you at the source
Where the tree's deepest roots drink from the abyss.

Nothing in the abyss is alien to you.
Sleep at the tree's root, where the night is spun
Into the stuff of worlds, listen to the winds,
The tides, and the night's harmonies, and know
All that you knew before you began to forget,
Before you became estranged from your own being,
Before you had too long parted from those other
More simple children, who have stayed at home
In meadow and island and forest, in sea and river.
Earth sends a mother's love after her exiled child,
Entrusting her message to the light and air,
The wind and waves that carry your ship, the rain that falls,
The birds that call to you, and all the shoals
That swim in the natal waters of her ocean.

At the Beginning

Fulani Oral Tradition

Author Unknown

This Fulani creation myth from northern Nigeria is the people's way of explaining the world and its origins. Doondari, who becomes Gueno at the end of the poem, is their creator god. The five elements at the beginning of the poem (stone, iron, fire, water, and air) are balanced against the five stages of humankind's suffering and final triumph.

At the beginning there was a huge drop of milk.
Then Doondari came and he created the stone.
Then the stone created iron,
And iron created fire,
And fire created water,
And water created air.

Then Doondari descended the second time,
And he took the five elements
And he shaped them into a human being.
But the human creature was proud,
So Doondari created blindness, and blindness defeated the creature.
But when blindness became too proud,
Doondari created sleep, and sleep defeat blindness.
But when sleep became too proud,
Doondari created worry, and worry defeated sleep.
But when worry became too proud,
Doondari created death, and death defeated worry.
But then death became too proud.

Doondari descended for the third time,
    and he came as Gueno, the eternal one,
    and Gueno defeated death.

Before God Created the World

A Sikh Creation Narrative

Apji Sahib and Rag Gaur Bairagan

The Sikh religion holds that the universe is composed of five elements: air, water, earth, fire, and space. Water is the father, Earth the mother. God, who brought everything into being, is a personal God who continues to nourish and sustain every aspect of creation.

Before God created the world there was no earth nor sky, nor sun or human; neither Brahma nor Vishnu. The cycle of birth and death, pleasure and pain and the sacred scriptures were all non-existent. No creatures, no humans, nothing at all existed. God alone existed in this Akhand Smadhi (unbroken trance) until he decided to create our world. God, the creator, brought all the worlds and the underworlds into existence through the Divine Word. Guru Nānak said, "God spoke once and there was creation.

For millions and millions of countless years was spread darkness when existed neither earth nor human but only the Limitless Divine Ordinance. Then existed neither day nor light nor sun nor moon. The Creator into unbroken trance was absorbed. Then were not Brahma, Vishnu or Shiva, none other than the sole God was visible. Neither existed then female or male or caste or birth. None suffering or joy received. Then were not instituted recitation of scripture or keeping of vows, fasts or worship offerings. Then, creating continents, spheres and nether worlds, the hidden God made himself manifest.

As their creator, the natural beauty which exists and can be found in all living things whether animals, birds, fish, belongs to God and God alone is their ruler. Without God's order, nothing exists, changes or develops.

Having brought the world into being, God sustains, nourishes and protects it. Nothing is overlooked. Even creatures in rocks and stones are well provided for. Birds who fly thousands of miles away leaving their young ones behind know that they will be sustained and taught to fend for themselves by God. The creatures of nature lead their lives under God's command and with God's grace. Guru Nānak applauds their closeness to God and his creation in this hymn:

> If I were a doe living in the forest, eating grass and leaves,
> with god's grace I would find God.
> If I were a cuckoo living in the mango tree,
> contemplating and singing,
> God would reveal divine mercy.
> If I were a female snake, dwelling in the ground,
> God's word would be in my being,
> my dread would vanish.
> Eternal God is found,
> light meets light.

Praise Belongs to God

Selected readings on Creation from the Koran (Interpreted)

Arthur John Arberry

The Koran is the book of Islam which is believed to have been revealed to the prophet Mohammed (c. 570-629) through the mediation of the archangel Gabriel. It is second only the Bible in its influence on Western civilization. Muslims believe that there is only one Koran, written in Arabic, which cannot be translated. Thus, any translations into other languages are considered interpretation. Arthur John Arberry's interpretation, first published in 1955, is still recognized as one of the most accurate. Asbury acquired a first-hand knowledge and appreciation of the Islamic world when he served as a classics professor at Cairo University.

Praise belongs to God
who created the heavens and the earth
and appointed the shadows and light. . . .
It is God who created you out of clay.
He is God in the heavens and the earth.

God created the sun and the moon,
each one running to a term stated.
It is the Holy One who stretched out the earth
and stretched therein
firm mountains and rivers,
and every fruit.

God is He that looses the winds
that stir up the dust. . . .
God created you of dust
then a sperm-drop.
Then He made you pairs.
Not equal are the two seas;
this one is gentle, grateful to taste,
delicious to drink,
and that is salt, bitter to the tongue.
Yet both you eat.

The cattle—
God created them for you;
in them is warmth, and uses various,
and of them you eat.
There is beauty in them for you,
when you bring them home to rest
and when you drive them forth abroad to pasture.
They bear your loads
unto a land that you would never reach.
Surely your God is All-clement, All-compassionate,
for He created horses, and mules and asses for you to ride.

Praise belongs to God,
Originator of the heavens and earth,
who appointed the angels to be messengers
having wings two, three and four,
increasing creation as he wills.

O people, remember God's blessing upon you;
is there any creator, apart from God,
who provides for you out of heaven and earth?
God's promise is true.

The Creation

James Weldon Johnson

The twentieth century African American poet, diplomat and anthologist of black culture, James Weldon Johnson (1871-1938), offers this interpretation of the Biblical creation narrative. "The Creation" is a sermon in verse, taken from Johnson's best-known work, God's Trombones, *published in 1927. These themes have parallels in all religious and cultural traditions.*

And God stepped out in space
And he looked around and said:
I'm lonely—
I'll make me a world.

And far as the eye of God could see
Darkness covered everything,
Blacker than a hundred midnights
Down in a cypress swamp.

Then God smiled,
And the light broke,
And the darkness rolled up on one side,
And the light stood shining on the other,
And God said: That's good!

Then God reached out and took the light in His hands,
And God rolled the light around in His hands
Until he made the sun;
And He set that sun a-blazing in the heavens.
And the light that was left from making the sun
God gathered it up in a shining ball
And flung it against the darkness,
Spangling the night with the moon and stars.
Then down between

The darkness and the light
He hurled the world:
And God said: That's good!

Then God himself stepped down—
And the Sun was on His right hand,
And the moon was on His left;
The stars were clustered about His head,
And Earth was under His feet.
And God walked, and where He trod
His footsteps hollowed the valleys out
And bulged the mountains up.

Then He stopped and looked and saw
That Earth was hot and barren.
So God stepped over the edge of the world
And He spat out the seven seas—
He batted His eyes, and the lightnings flashed—
He clapped His hands, and the thunders rolled—
And the waters above Earth came down,
The cooling waters came down.

Then the green grass sprouted,
And the little red flowers blossomed,
The pine tree pointed his finger to the sky,
And the oak spread out his arms,
The lakes cuddled down in the hollows of the ground,
And the rivers ran down to the sea;
And God smiled again.
And the rainbow appeared,
And curled itself around His shoulder.

Then God raised His arm and He waved His hand
Over the sea and over the land,
And He said: Bring forth! Bring forth!

And quicker than God could drop His hand,
Fishes and fowls,
And beasts and birds
Swam the rivers and the seas,
Roamed the forests and the woods,
And split the air with their wings,
And God said: That's good!

Then God walked around,
And God looked around
On all that He had made.
He looked at His sun,
And He looked at His moon,
And He looked at His little stars;
He looked on His world
With all its living things,
And God said: I'm lonely still.

Then God sat down—
On the side of a hill where He could think;
By a deep, wide river He sat down;
With His head in His hands,
God thought and thought,
Till He thought: I'll make me a man!

Up from the bed of the river
God scooped the clay;
And by the bank of the river
He kneeled Him down;
And there the great God Almighty
Who lit the sun and fixed it in the sky,
Who flung the stars to the most far corner of the night,
Who rounded Earth in the middle of His hand;
This Great God,
Like a mammy bending over her baby,

Kneeled down in the dust
Toiling over a lump of clay
Till He shaped it in His own image.
Then into it He blew the breath of life,
And man became a living soul.
Amen. Amen.

Creation Story: A Retelling

"In the beginning was the Word, and the Word was with God, and the Word was God." —*John 1:1*

Moyra Caldecott

Usually Christians look to the Book of Genesis for a biblical account of creation, yet Moyra Caldecott has used the opening verse of St. John's Gospel to great effect in inviting us to marvel, in the present tense, at the wonder of creation and the immensity of time it is taking for the "Great Work" to come into being.

Outside Time the Consciousness of God exists.
In that Consciousness
is a thought
of such intensity that within it
all and everything
conceivable and inconceivable,
imaginable and unimaginable,
possible and impossible
is contained.
That thought is uttered
and from the vibrations of that sound,
from the resonance of that Word,
from what the scientists call
"The Big Bang,"

the multitudinous forms of being are spreading
in ever increasing circles.

The vast universe of whirling forms takes shape.
World after world swings through space,
each to each held
by an inner and invisible force,
the whole
a balance of attraction and repulsion.
Within these worlds
light and dark interact.
Eons pass.
Liquid fire cools to rock,
scalding steam to rain.
More than a thousand million years pass.
More than a thousand million times
the burning orb of the sun rises and sets
over the desolate landscapes of our earth—
its powerful cosmic rays ever active, ever potent.

Cautiously the first life forms emerge—
infinitesimal cells divide, join up with others,
subdivide, rejoin.
The liquid oceans seethe with life.
Beings with or without calcareous shells
live and die by their billions
trilobites
graptolites
brachiopods
drifting through the waters for three hundred million years
to lie at last on the ancient sea bed,
their minute bodies
forming the fossiliferous rock
we walk so casually upon today,
while the shell of the ammonite

that pumped through the primal ocean
so vigorously in search of food
has been replaced molecule by molecule by crystal
and lies now, bejeweled, in our museums,
curled, whorled and spiraled.
Some life-forms collect in rock pools,
breathe air,
grow and change.
The first fish struggle on to land
exchanging fins for limbs.
Corals and sponges build their sturdy tenements
and learn communal living in the oceans.

On land, cold-blooded reptiles sun themselves singly
upon the rocks,
mosses and horsetail plants as tall as forest trees
flourish in the marshlands.
Three hundred and fifty million years ago
the coal beds formed as these marshland forests died.
Another two hundred million years
and the dinosaurs tread hot sand
leaving their giant footsteps, fossilized.
Where have they gone, these ancient fearsome beasts?
They with the tiny ammonites and belemnites are now extinct.
Do we still carry them in our blood?
Time moves on.
Small warm-blooded mammals take their place
among the cycads, gingkoes, ferns and conifers.
Birds sing
and the first flowering plants put out their finery.
Another sixty million years go by
and we rise to our feet,
lift our eyes to the firmament
and begin to name names
and recognize our God.

Still with us
is the first impetus of the Word.
Our being is the expression of God's Thought.
We contain the love of God and God contains us
and as we unfold on earth
through shell-creature,
fish-form,
reptile,
bird
and mammal—
through ichthyosaurs
plesiosaurs
dinosaurs
and ape—
we are learning
step by step
what that containment means.

The circles are still widening—
still evolving the mighty concept—
the magnificent Idea.
Six days,
Seven . . .
a million years,
a thousand million . . .
the count is nothing,
the Being—All.
Praise be to our great God
and the Word that resonates
in our hearts still.
May we not separate ourselves in arrogance
from the Great Work
for we know the sound of the Word
but not its full meaning.

O Creating God Who Spreads the Earth, Forgive Us and Love Us

Rig Veda

Interpreted by the Writers Workshop of Calcutta, India

From the Rig Veda, *one of the four core Hindu scriptures, this prayer is to Varuna, the sky god. Hindus understand God as the one supreme principle of the universe who is approached through a variety of names. Hinduism is the world's most ancient religion and the third largest. It does not have one identifiable founder; it is a fusion of historical traditions, which have taken root in the soil of India.*

O Creating God,
who spreads the earth like a carpet for the sun,
like the skin of a sacrificed beast,
listen to our prayer.

O Creating God,
who places the winds in the forests,
puts wings on horses, milk in cows, virtue in human beings,
who puts fish in the waters, sun in the sky, wind in the mountains,

O Creating God,
who tilts the cup of the clouds on the three worlds,
heaven, earth and middle sky,
lord who drenches fields of barley with rain,

O Creating God,
who floods earth and sky with sweet milk
when hills are clothed with cloud
and the storms come rushing,

We sing to your glory, O Creating God:
You stand in the universe,
You hold it in your power,
You measure the earth with the sun.

We do not question your power, O Wise God,
like shining rivers that flow, and flowing
do not fill the sea
into which they flow. . . .

If we have ever sinned against a friend,
if we have ever sinned against a brother or sister, mother or father,
if we have sinned against neighbor or stranger,
O Forgiving God, forgive us.

If, like gamblers at dice, we have cheated,
cheated knowingly or unknowingly,
O forgiving God, forgive us.
Forgive us, restore us and love us.

II

Earth, Our Mother

We were flying over America and suddenly I saw snow, the first snow we ever saw from orbit, and then it struck me that we are all children of the Earth. It does not matter what country you look at. We are all Earth's children, and we should treat her as our mother.

—Aleksandr Aleksandrov,

Russian cosmonaut

Nature We See

Guru Nānak

The Sikh religion, a hybrid of Islam and Hinduism, was founded by Guru Nānak (1469-1539), from the Punjab region of northwest India. Sikhism has been built on the message of the oneness of creation. The Sikh holy book, from which this selection is taken, is called the Guru Granth Sahib; *it is a collection of the wisdom of the first ten gurus of Sikhism.*

Nature we see
Nature we hear
Nature we observe with awe, wonder and joy
Nature in nether regions
Nature in the skies
Nature in the whole creation
Nature in the sacred texts
Nature in all reflection
Nature in food, in water, in garments and in love for all
Nature in species, kinds, colors
Nature in life forms
Nature in good deeds
Nature in pride and in ego
Nature in air, water and fire
Nature in the soil of the earth.
All nature is yours, O powerful Creator,
You command it, observe it and pervade within it.

Every Part of the Earth Is Sacred

Chief Seattle

Chief Seattle, in this letter written to President James Polk in 1852, explains that the holiness of all creation is revealed in the web and unity of mutually dependent relationships. This eloquent statement has been described as the most beautiful and profound treatise ever rendered on the environment. "None of us can be apart. We are all brothers and sisters, woven together into this sacred earth."

Every part of the earth is sacred to my people. Every shining pine needle, every sandy shore, every mist in the dark woods, every meadow, every humming insect. All are holy.

We know the sap that courses through the trees as we know the blood that runs though our veins. We are part of the earth and the earth is part of us. The perfumed flowers are our sisters. The bear, the deer, the great eagle; these are our brothers. The rocky crests, the berries in the meadow, the body heat of the pony and the people, all belong to the same family.

The shining water that moves in the streams and rivers is not just water but the blood of our ancestors. Each shimmering reflection in the clear water of the lakes tells of events and memories in the life of my people. The water's murmur is the voice of my father's father.

The rivers are our brothers. They quench our thirst. They carry our canoes and give drink to our children. So you must give the rivers the kindness you would give any brother or sister.

The air is precious to us. The air shares its spirit with all the life it supports. The wind that gave our grandfather his first breath also receives his last sigh. The wind also gives our children the spirit of life.

The earth is our mother. What befalls the earth befalls all the children of the earth. All things are connected like the blood that connects us all. We did not weave the web of life, we are merely strands in it.

Whatever we do to the web, we do to ourselves.

This we know: that our god is also your god. The earth is precious to God and to harm the earth is to heap contempt upon its creator.

What will happen when the buffalo are all slaughtered? The wild horses tamed? What will happen when the secret corners of the forest are heavy with the scent of many people and the view of the ripe hills is blotted by talking wires? Where will the thicket be? Gone! Where will the eagle be? Gone! And what is it to say good-bye to the swift pony and the hunt? The end of living and the beginning of survival.

We love the earth as a newborn loves its mother's heartbeat. Preserve the land for all children and love it, as God loves us all. We Indians are part of this land. You too are part of this land. The earth is precious to us. It is also precious to you. None of us can be apart. We are all brothers and sisters, together woven in to this sacred earth.

Everything in Nature Bespeaks the Mother — Kahlil Gibran

Kahlil Gibran (1883-1931), the Lebanese-American artist and writer, became a household name in the 1960s with the discovery of his book, The Prophet, *published in 1923 and translated into more than twenty languages. Gibran was a complex man who did not live the serene life suggested by* The Prophet. *Nonetheless, his amaranthine words are still as contemporary as they were when they were originally published in Arabic in 1912.*

Everything in nature bespeaks the mother. The sun is the mother of earth and gives its nourishment of heat. It never leaves the universe at night until it has put the earth to sleep to the song of the sea and the hymn of birds and brooks. And this earth is the mother of trees and flowers. It produces them, nurses them, and weans them. The trees and flowers become kind mothers of their great fruits and seeds. And the mother, the prototype of all existence, is the eternal spirit, full of beauty and love.

A Land of Flowing Streams

Deuteronomy 8

Paraphrase by Anne Rowthorn

The Hebrews had great affection for the land and they integrated this love with a comprehensive moral framework. In this selection, the Hebrews are entering Canaan, the "Promised Land," a land flowing with milk and honey. The generous God who provides such abundance only requires in return that the people honor the Divine Power and "not forget your Creator by failing to keep God's commandments."

Your gracious God is bringing you into a good land, a land with flowing streams gushing out into the valleys and hills. God is leading you to a land full of wheat and barley, of vines and fig trees and pomegranates, a land of olive trees and honey. It is a land where you will eat bread without scarcity, where you will lack nothing, a land whose stones are iron and from whose hills you may mine copper. You shall eat your fill and bless your God for the good land the Holy One has given you.

But take care that you do not forget your Creator by failing to keep God's commandments. Do not forget that is was God who led you through the great and terrible wilderness, who made water flow for you from a rock and fed you in the wilderness.

God of the Earth, Our Mother, Make a Wide World for Us

Hymn to the Earth

Abridged and Adapted by Anne Rowthorn

"God of the Earth, Our Mother, Make a Wide World for Us" comes from the latest of the four Hindu vedas (sacred books of knowledge). It is a beautiful, comprehensive prayer of petition to God to make a wide world for humanity, to abundantly supply cattle and crops, and to bestow upon earth fruitful harvests. It asks God to protect the earth's natural resources and to keep human beings from harming her. This selection is rich in feminine imagery, concluding in the final stanza with, "May the God of the Earth give us the milk of her blessing," and "Earth, our mother, set us on the paths of peace in full accord with Heaven."

Truth, eternal order, that is great and stern,
holiness, austerity, prayer and ritual—
these uphold the Earth.
May you, queen of what has been and will be,
make a wide world for us.

Earth which has many heights and slopes and
unconfined plain that binds everything together,
Earth that bears plants with healing powers,
may you spread wide for us and thrive.

Earth, in which lie the sea, the rivers and other waters,
in which food and cornfields have come to be,
In which live all that breathes and that moves,
may you confer on us the finest of your yield.

Guardian of the four quarters, in whom
food and cornfields have come to be,
who bears in many forms the breathing and moving life,
may you give us cattle and crops.

Earth, in which people of old before us
performed their varied works,
Where good overwhelms evil,
Earth, the home of all living things—
may you give us magnificent grace.

All sustaining, treasure-bearing, firm foundation,
home of all moving life,
Earth bears the sacred universal fire.
May you, God Almighty, protect its wealth.

Earth, whom the celestial guardians protect forever without erring,
may you, God of the Earth, pour on us your sweet blessings
and endow us with joy.

Earth, which at first was in the water of the ocean;
Earth whose spirit is in the eternal Heaven,
wrapped in truth immortal,
May you give us wisdom.

Earth, in which the waters, common to all,
moving on all sides, flowing unfailing, day and night;
May you pour on us milk of many streams,
like a mother to her child,
and endow us with constancy.

Pleasant be your hills, O Earth,
your snow-clad mountains and your woods!
Oh Earth—brown, black, red and multi-colored—
the firm Earth protected by God,
on this Earth may we stand, unvanquished, unslain, unharmed.

Set us, O Earth, amidst what is your center and your navel,
    and the life-giving forces that emanate from you.
Purify us from all sides.
Earth, you are our mother, we your children:
    Give us rain in due season and fill us with your plenty.

The evil ones who threaten the Earth
    with malevolent thoughts and weapons of destruction,
Overwhelm them, O God of the Earth, as you have done before.

Born of you and on you move every living creature;
    you bear them all—the two legged and four legged.
Yours, O Earth, are all the races of humanity
    on whom the sun rises and spreads with its rays of light immortal.
In concert, may all creatures pour out unending thanksgivings.

Mother of all plants,
    firm Earth upheld by eternal law,
May you be ever beneficent and gracious to us,
    as we tread upon your lands.

A vast abode you are, and mighty,
    strong is your speed, your moving and your shaking.
You, all powerful God, protect us without ceasing.
May you, O Earth, make us shine forth
    with the brightness of your radiance.

A fire lies deep within the Earth.
    It is in plants and waters and stone.
There is a fire deep within the people,
    a fire in the kilns and a fire in horses.
This is the same fire that burns in the heavens;
    all fire belongs to this Fire Divine.

People of Earth kindle this fire and bear their oblations.
May Earth, clad in her fiery mantle, fire us
  and light our ways.

The fragrance that rises from you, O Earth
  is carried in plants and in the waters.
God of the Earth, protect us with your sweetness and grace.

Rock, soil, stone and dust by which
  Earth is held together and bound firm;
To you, O God of the Earth, we offer our devotion.

Rising or sitting, standing or walking,
  may we, neither with our right foot or our left,
  ever totter on the earth.

Earth, purifier, patient Earth,
  bearer of power, and plenty.
  sharer of food and molten butter;
May we grow strong through your spiritual might.

May those that are of the eastern regions,
  and the northern and the southern and the western,
  be gentle as they walk upon the Earth.
Protect us from stumbling while we walk upon your world.
As you guide our steps, keep us from being pushed as from the West or from the East, or from the North or from the South.
Keep us on the straight path so that we may not wander astray.

As long as we look on you from around, O Earth,
  with the sun as friend,
So long as year follows year,
  may our vision not fail.
When we are lying down, O Earth,
  protect us and all who sleep.

Whatever I dig from you, O Earth,
may your mantle grow back again quickly.
O Earth, purifier, may we never injure you.

May your summer, O Earth, and your rains,
your autumn, your dewy months, your winters and your spring,
May these seasons, Earth, that make the year,
and day and night
pour their abundance upon us.

Earth in which are cities, the works of God
and fields where people are variously employed;
Earth that bears all things in her womb,
may you, O Lord of Life, make us graceful from every side.

The people of the Earth speak a multitude of tongues,
they have a variety of religious rites,
according to their places of abode,
Pour upon us all your treasure in a thousand streams,
like a cow full of milk that never fails.

The snake and the scorpion with the sharp sting that,
overpowered by the cold season, lie bewildered in the caves,
The worm and each thing that comes to life, O Earth,
and moves about with the coming on of rains,
may these, creeping things, never creep near us.

Your many pathways for folk to travel on,
the roads for chariots, and for wagons to pass through,
On which walk together both the good and the evil,
may no dangers overcome us, and may thieves and foes be driven
far from us.

Your forest animals and wild beasts of the woods—
    lions, tigers, man-eaters that prowl about,
The hyena, the wolf and the bear,
    keep these, O God of the Earth, far away from us.

Earth in which the winged birds fly together—
    swans, eagles and other birds of various kinds,
    on which the wind blows strong, raising the dust, bending trees,
Earth in which night and day—the black and the bright in union—
    are settled, Earth which is covered over by rain—
May you, God of all the Earth,
    establish your peace in every home.

In villages, in the forest and in the assemblies on the earth,
    in congregations and in councils, may we speak of
    you, God of Earth, in reverent terms.

As a horse scatters dust, so did Earth, since she was born,
    scatter the people who dwelt on the land,
    and she joyously sped on, the world's protector,
    supporter of forest trees and plants.

Peaceful, sweet-smelling, gracious, filled with milk,
    and bearing nectar,
May the God of the Earth give to us the milk of her blessing.
Bearers of your bounty may our lives be lives of unceasing thanksgivings
  for all the blessings of the Earth.
Earth, our mother, set us on the paths of peace in full accord with
  Heaven.
Holy God, Wise One Immortal, forever keep your Earth in grace and
  splendor.

Every Being in the Universe

Lao-Tzu

Nothing is known about Lao-Tzu (c. 571 B.C.E.) except that he left behind him a book of eighty-one chapters which for the last 2,000 years have been called Tao Te Ching. *This modest little book bred Taoism and deeply influenced Buddhism; it led to Ch'an and Zen meditation and inspired Chinese poetry and landscape painting. For centuries it was Asia's most widely read book; and it continues to serve as a guide for persons in search for the universal meaning of existence.*

Every being in the universe
Is an expression of God.
All life springs into existence,
unconscious,
perfect,
free,
taking on shapes,
letting circumstances
bring it to completion.

God gives birth to all things,
nourishes them,
maintains them,
cares for them,
comforts them,
protects them,
takes them back to herself,
creating without possessing,
acting without expecting,
guiding without interfering.

This is why the
love of God
is in the very nature of things,
in every being in the universe.

Earth, Sister Earth

Helder Camara

Dom Helder Camara (1909-1999), Archbishop of Olinda and Recife, the poorest and least developed region of Brazil, was beloved as an uncompromising champion of human rights. The Earth, created by the one loving, just, and compassionate God was Dom Helder Camara's first point of reference and provided the foundation of his life, faith and action. "Earth, Sister Earth" is the first of a series of poems in which the poet identifies with the Earth and speaks as from the Earth herself.

Teach us
To continue the Creation
To help the seeds
To multiply,
Giving food
For the people
And for the beasts.

Teach us
To further the joy
You never tire of offering
When weary travelers find you,
A signpost to their home.

Teach us
To make the horizon
Become a beautiful image
Of Creation's grandeur.

Teach us
To accept
The meditation of those
Who wish to unite us
To our fellows,
As we accept the gift
Of the water that binds
Land to land,
No matter how great the distances!

What do you suffer
In the dust of the deserts?
How do you look upon
Those of us who,
Though capable of transforming
The waste to lushness,
Prefer to be creators
Of barrenness?

And how do you rejoice
In the rain
That brings forth your fruits?
And what pain do you feel
At the storms
That drown you with floods,
Destroying plantations,
Crushing houses and lives
Of animals, of plants, of people?

How great is the lesson
You give us,
O Earth,
More than sister:
Our Mother Earth!

All our lives
We walk carelessly across you,
And when life leaves us,
With no shadow of resentment,
You open up to us
Your maternal bosom
To keep our flesh,
Our ashes,
For the joy
Of the resurrection.

Awe and Adoration

Once in a while
you may come across a place
where everything
seems as close to perfection
as you will ever need.

—Brian Turner,
"Place"

God's World

Edna St. Vincent Millay

Born in Rockland, Maine, the Pulitzer Prize winning poet, Edna St. Vincent Millay (1892-1952), was already a published poet by the time she was fifteen. She went to Vassar College and lived a stylish life, among artists and writers in Greenwich Village and in Paris. One imagines this poem being written on a visit home to the tough, craggy Maine coast on a brilliant autumn day. How often have we, like the poet, been so entranced by a ravishing day that we feel we want to embrace it?

O world, I cannot hold thee close enough!
    Thy winds, thy wide grey skies!
    Thy mists that roll and rise!
Thy woods, this autumn day, that ache and sag
And all but cry with color! That gaunt crag
To crush! To lift the lean of that black bluff!
World, World, I cannot get thee close enough!

Long have I known the glory in it all,
    But never I knew this;
    Here such a passion is
As stretched me apart. Lord, I do not fear
Thou'st made the world too beautiful this year.
My soul is all but out of me,—let fall
No burning leaf; prithee, let no bird call.

The Glory of the Forest Meadows is the Lily

John Muir

The Apostle of the Wilderness, John Muir (1838-1914) kept a diary during his first visit to Yosemite and its environs in 1869. Upon first encountering the Sierra Nevada Mountains, Muir experienced a spiritual awakening and he urged others to put themselves in the circumstances where they could do the same. "Climb the mountains and get the good tidings. Nature's peace will flow into you as sunshine flows into trees. The winds will blow their freshness into you, and the storms their energy, while cares will drop off as autumn leaves."

The glory of the forest meadow is the lily. The tallest are from seven to eight feet high with magnificent racemes (stems) of ten to twenty or more small orange-colored flowers. They stand out free in open ground, with just enough grass and other companion plants about them to fringe their feet, and how them off to best advantage.

After how many centuries of Nature's care planting and watering them, tucking the bulbs in snugly below winter's frost, shading the tender shoots with clouds drawn above them like curtains, pouring refreshing rain, making them perfect in beauty, and keeping them safe by a thousand miracles. So extravagant is Nature with her choicest treasures, spending plant beauty as she spends sunshine, pouring it forth into land and sea, garden and desert. And so the beauty of lilies falls on angels and men, bears and squirrels, wolves and sheep, birds and bees.

I Believe a Leaf of Grass . . .

Walt Whitman

"I Believe a Leaf of Grass" is an extract from a sweeping fifty-two stanza poem entitled "Song of Myself." Walt Whitman (1819-1892) is at one and the same time both irreverent and refreshing. Although he was never considered a poet of nature, this excerpt illustrates Whitman's sharp powers of observation and his appreciation of the natural world. Leaves of Grass, *published in 1855, won Emerson's acclaim and almost immediately established Whitman's reputation as a writer.*

I believe a leaf of grass is no less than the journeywork of the stars,
And the pismire is equally perfect, and a grain of sand,
    and the egg of the wren,
And the tree toad is a chef-d'oeuvre for the highest,
And the running blackberry would adorn the parlors of heaven,
And the narrowest hinge in my hand puts to scorn all machinery,
And the cow crunching with depressed head surpasses any statue,
And a mouse is miracle enough to stagger sextillions of infidels.
I find I incorporate gneiss, coal, long-threaded moss, fruits,
    grains, succulent roots,
And am stuccoed with quadrupeds and birds all over,
And have distanced what is behind me for good reasons,
But call anything back again when I desire it.
In vain the plutonic rocks send their old heat against my approach,
In vain the mastodon retreats beneath its own powdered,
In vain objects stand leagues off and assume manifold shapes,
In vain the ocean settling in hollows and the great monsters lying low,
In vain the buzzard houses herself with the sky,
In vain the snake slides through the creepers and logs,
In vain the elk takes to the inner passes of the woods,
In vain the razor-billed auk sails far north to Labrador,
I follow quickly, I ascend to the nest in the fissure of the cliff.
I think I could turn and live with animals, they are so placid
    and self-contained,

I stand and look at them long and long.
They do not sweat and whine about their condition,
They do not lie awake in the dark and weep for their sins,
They do not make me sick discussing their duty to God,
Not one is dissatisfied, not one is demented with the
    mania of owning things,
Not one kneels to one another, nor to this kind that lived thousands
    of years ago,
Not one is respectable or unhappy over the whole earth.
So they show their relations to me and I accept them,
They bring me tokens of myself . . .

More Than Resonance and Echo

Catherine de Vinck

The contemporary poet, Catherine de Vinck, asks the primeval question, "Where are we going?", and she implies that if we do not know, we can take strength in the knowledge that the hawks and vultures, the wild grapes and ferns come and go in their season, suggesting that the natural world will ultimately survive the ravages of human beings.

Ferns, climbing vines, wild grapes
  such is reality, seen, touched, tasted.
What we hear
  voices of the wind rasping through the pines
  bird-calls looped through the leaves
Come to us clearly, each sound
  with its own shape and modulation.
Is there more to the world
  Than this triangle of sky
  observed through the window?

From where did we come?
  Spawned from star-dust, born in water
  carried in the salty arms of the sea?
We begin as shapeless nouns
  Soft bones, wet skin
waiting for the incandescent verbs
  to activate our lives.
Can we say anything new
  anything that will fill the mind
  with pure helium, lifted it high
  above itself
    a balloon of many colors?

Where are we going? The hawks know:
    The vultures in their mourning coats know;
The roots coiled under the porch
    know how all things recede
    break upon mending;
how the center trembles and dissolves
    away from itself forever.
Handful of ashes, papery scraps
    Is that the evidence at the end?

We are more than resonance and echo
    more than movement and speech.
What is gone from us, what is lost
    returns, is returned: a new earth
Ferns, climbing vines, wild grapes
    in an otherness of place
    now hidden from mortal eyes.

A Quiet Temple Thick Set With Flowers

Selected lines and stanza

Li Po

The works of the great wandering poet of the T'ang Dynasty, Li Po (701-762), transmit a feeling of intimacy that leaps across centuries and cultures. The reader is not outside the poetry but swept up in the beauty described, finding new strength and happiness by identifying with its richness. When we are successful in making this identification, we will become like the gentle rain which ". . . showers its blessings, silently, softly, upon everything."

A quiet temple thick set with flowers;
A sequestered lake hidden in the fine bamboos.

What a lovely patch of green!
I know it's grass on the other side of the lake.
What a glorious stretch of crimson!
I see it's clouds beyond the eastern sea.

A tortoise leaves a watery patch behind it,
As it sails slowly through the duckweeds.

Kingfishers are chirping on a clothesline.
A dragonfly rests motionless on the silken cord of a fishing rod.

Entering into the peach blossoms,
Redness grows soft and tender.
Returning to the willow leaves,
Greenness becomes fresh and new.

The dark ravine oozes with the music of silence.
The bright moonlight is being sifted through the thick foliage.

A tiny rivulet trickles like a hidden thread through a flower path.
Spring stars girdle my grass hut like a necklace of pearls.

The emeraldine fine bamboos, in the gentle caress of the wind,
The red water lilies, bathed in the rain,
Send forth whiff after whiff of invisible incense.

Countless dragonflies are darting up and down in a group.
A pair of wild ducks float and dive together.

White sandy beaches and emerald bamboos
Embrace the river village in eventide.
The wooden door of my humble house
Seems to hold a hearty tête-à-tête with the new moon.

The autumn water is clear and fathomless.
It cleanses and refreshes the heart of the lonely traveler.

The peach blossoms and pear blossoms
Follow closely upon one another's heels to the ground.
The yellow birds and white birds
Sometimes mingle together in their flight.

The birds are whiter for the blue of the river;
The flowers almost burn on the green hills.

Darting upwards, a bee gets tangled in a falling catkin.
Forming a line, the ants are crawling up to a withered pear.

A gentle shower, and the little fish come to the surface;
The waters being deep, the fish are extremely happy.

The maples and orange trees,
Are playing for us a wonderful orchestra of colors!
The evening sun is smoking the fine grass.
The luminous river is sparkling through the screen.

The forest being thick, the birds feel right at home.
A little breeze, and the swallows are darting with slanting wings.

In the depth of the night the temple strikes me with a sudden awe.
The tinkling of the golden bells by the wind brings silence to the fore.
Blackness has enveloped the courtyard with all its spring colors.
Dark fragrance is haunting this stainless spot on earth.

The nice rain knows its season,
It is born of Spring.
It follows the wind secretly into the night,
And showers its blessings, silently, softly, upon everything.

Leisure

W. D. Davies

The Welsh poet, W. D. Davies (1871-1940) worked his way around Europe supporting himself as a wrangler, a picker of fruit, and by odd job that came to hand. He lost a leg jumping a train in Canada but got a wooden replacement and kept on going. He wrote about his adventures in Autobiography of a Supertramp, *which came out in 1908 with a preface by George Bernard Shaw. "Leisure" is his best-known poem.*

What is this life if, full of care,
We have no time to stand and stare.
No time to stand beneath the boughs
And stare as long as sheep or cows.
No time to see, when woods we pass,
Where squirrels hide their nuts in grass.
No time to see, in broad daylight,
Streams full of stars, like skies at night.
No time to turn at Beauty's glance,
And watch her feet, how they can dance.
No time to wait till her mouth can
Enrich that smile her eyes began.
A poor life this is if, full of care,
We have no time to stand and stare.

Moments of Rising Mist

Poets of the Sung Dynasty

Translated by Amitendranath Tagore

We do not know the names of Chinese landscape poets of the Sung Dynasty (960-1279) who wrote these poems. Both painting and poetry flourished during this vibrant era; many of the great painters of the age were also poets. They believed that to know the place of human beings in the totality of the universe was the height of wisdom.

You look but cannot reach,
You walk, the road goes twisting.
A path appears on the wood tip;
A thousand cliffs are visible beneath the clouds.
Fog and mist gleamed, now it is dark again.
The last glow lingers on the peak's tip.

Waterfall echoes amidst the spring cliff,
Night is deep, the mountain is already quiet.
Bright moon washes the pine forest,
All the peaks are the same tint.

Summer rain makes the forest muddy;
Slanting sunbeams reflect again and again.
Pure green, no wind ruffles it;
Let the spring grass smile!

Thousands of ridges stab at the clouds;
One glance is not enough.
Frontal ranges and the distant peaks,
Purplish blue, deep and light.

Enter the path and view the stone gate,
A vague green amidst the deep cloudy sky.
Clouds appear between the smooth stone steps,
Old trees and cold heavenly breeze.
Look at the last sun-glow; listen to the mountain cicadas.

In This World

Selected Haiku from the Works of Issa

Translated by Robert Hass

Issa (1763-1827) was a farmer's son born in a small mountain village in central Japan. Like Bashō and Buson, he went to Edo to study poetry and three years later became the master of his poetry center. He studied Buddhism, became a monk, and then began an itinerant life. Issa was particularly fond of the smallest creatures—flies, fleas, crickets, even bed bugs and lice.

In this world—
we walk on the roof of hell,
gazing at flowers.

A good world—
the dewdrops fall
by ones, by twos.

Crescent moon—
bent to the shape
of the cold.

The cuckoo sings
to me, to the mountain,
to me, to the mountain.

New Year's morning:
the ducks on the pond
quack and quack.

The evening clears—
on the pale sky
row on row of autumn mountains.

Insects on a bough
floating downriver,
still singing.

Something Greater Than Heaven

Seuk Ho

Seuk Ho (b. 1934) first made his name as a young poet living in Taiwan writing in Chinese in the 1960s. He began writing in Korean in 1969. Ho's themes are taken from nature. Here, he asks the universal question—Who calls me?—and invites us to do the same.

Who calls me
that I go into barren emptiness
only to find a wind in the hollow corner
burrowing into the earholes of dandelions?

Who calls me
that I stand on the grass
where the crescent moon is moored while
I hear the dews dropping down
captured in the starry field all night long?

Who calls me
that when I feel the rail of dusking twilight
I hear the skeletons of leaves fallen last year
undulate their waists for a crawl?

Who calls me
that I cannot hear a sound
greater than the bell-sound when I come close to the hill
where the bell sounds?

Who calls me
as I go farther into emptiness
I find something greater emptied
something greater than heaven emptied—

Brother Fire

Helder Camara

On a blistering hot August day in 2008, forest fires are burning out of control in every western state; five million acres go up in smoke, the end of the burning nowhere in sight. How do we reconcile such tremendous destructive force with the idea that "all things work to the glory of God?"

Are you aware
Of your beauty?
Are you aware
Of the artless grace
With which you fulfill
Your high task
To conquer the dark?

Who taught
Your flames to leap,
O dancer's envy,
Light of step,
Spinning in long pirouettes
None can forget?

Often you have the pain
To offer human life
As a sacrifice through
Your touch of flame.

How do you find the courage
At such times, as you rise
In impetuous strength,
To give battle to the water;
And what are your thoughts
Of the humble, noble fire-fighter?

With simplicity
You feed the wood stove
And prepare the modest meals of
The families of the poor.

Do you not tremble with horror
When they speak of you
As a sign of punishment?
Yet with great respect
Do you consume and transfigure
The bodies of the martyrs!

Thank you Brother Fire,
For the warmth of your bring
To freezing bodies
Which have only you
As their help and salvation.

Thank you Brother Fire
For teaching us
To have a warm heart,
And helping us avoid
The emptiness of
A heart cold as stone.

Thank you Brother Fire
For the song in your flames
When, overcoming the darkness,
You become praise most pure
For our Father and Creator.

IV

The Web of Life

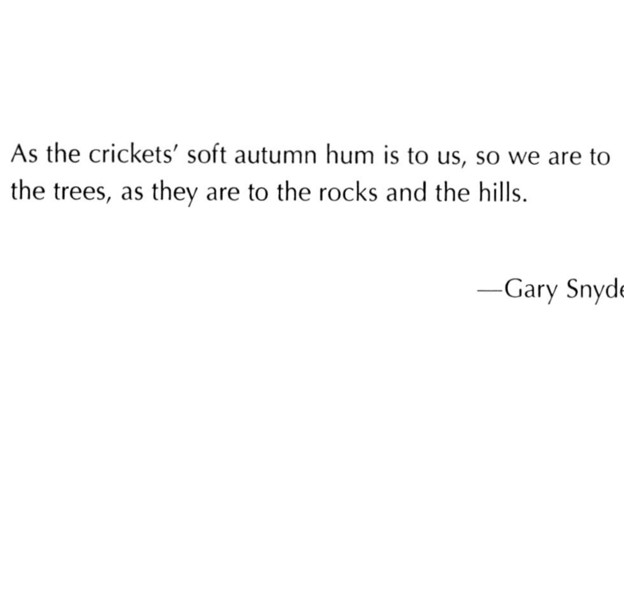

As the crickets' soft autumn hum is to us, so we are to the trees, as they are to the rocks and the hills.

—Gary Snyder

The Earth Is Alive

Andrea Cohen-Kiener

Rabbi Andrea Cohen-Kiener is the spiritual leader of P'nai or, a Jewish renewal congregation, and is the director of the Interreligious Eco-Justice Network in Connecticut. Andrea has a warm, passionate heart; she feels deeply for all her sisters and brothers, including Mother Earth and her creatures, as this poem amply illustrates.

The Earth is Alive and she breathes
The winds of the world and the leaves of the vegetation;
The gills of fish and the brachia of all species, these are the breath of the earth.

The Earth is Alive and she eats.
The bacteria of the soil and the guts of worms;
The teeth and flesh and bowels of all life, these are the digestive track of the earth.

The Earth is Alive and she has a circulatory system.
The waterways and aquifers, the clouds and the rain,
The pulse and blood of all life—these are the circulatory system of the earth.

The Earth is Alive and she knows.
The nervous system of all beings,
The frontal lobes of higher mammals—these are the earth's capacity to know herself.

The Earth is Alive and she eats.
The diminished range of species and the engineered seeds,
Captive livestock and roadside carrion, these are the digestive system of the earth.
The Earth is Alive and she has a circulatory system.
The Draino and detergents in our drains,
The acid and metals in our gentle rain, these infuse the bloodstream of the earth.

The Earth is Alive and she thinks.
The discomfort in our guts,
The smallness of our spirit,
The desolation of our disconnection—
These are earth's capacity to know herself.

We are then thought of the earth.

Widening Our Circle of Compassion

Albert Einstein

World-wide fame came in 1919 to the German-American physicist, Albert Einstein (1879-1955), when the theory of relativity which he developed was verified. Two years later he was awarded the Nobel Prize for Physics. In addition to Einstein's ground-breaking work in physics, he was deeply committed to charitable and social organizations which helped resettle large number of refugees arriving in the United States from Nazi Germany.

A human being is part of the whole . . . the universe. We experience thoughts and feelings, as something separated from the rest—a kind of optical delusion of consciousness. The delusion is a kind of prison for us, restricting us to our personal desires and to affection for a few persons nearest to us. Our task must be to free ourselves from this prison by widening our circle of compassion to embrace all living creatures and the whole of nature in its beauty.

Touch the Earth

Luther Standing Bear

The Lakota Indian, Luther Standing Bear, was born in 1868 and grew up on the high plains of what are now the states of North and South Dakota and Nebraska. He later became a chief. In this selection, he describes how the Lakota lived in kinship with all living creatures and why people need to touch the earth to be truly wise and truly human.

The Lakotas were true naturalists, lovers of nature. They loved the earth and all things of the earth, the attachment growing with age. The old people came literally to love the soil and they sat or reclined on the ground with a feeling of being close to a mothering power. It was good for the skin to touch the earth and the old people liked to remove their moccasins and walk with bare feet on the sacred earth. Their tipis were build on the earth and their altars were made of earth. The birds that flew in the air came to rest upon the earth and it was the final abiding place of all things that lived and grew. The soil was soothing, strengthening, cleansing and healing.

That is why the old Indians still sits upon the earth instead of propping themselves up and away from its life-giving forces. For them to sit or lie upon the ground is to be able to think more deeply and to feel more keenly; they can see more clearly into the mysteries of life and come closer in kinship to other lives around them . . .

Kinship with all creatures of the earth, sky and water was a real and active principle. For the animal and bird world there existed a familial feeling that kept the Lakota safe among them and so close did some of the Lakotas come to their feathered and furred friends that in true brotherhood they spoke a common tongue.

The old Lakotas were wise. They knew that a person's heart away from nature would become hard. They knew that lack of respect for growing and living things soon led to lack of respect for humans too. So they kept their youth close to the earth's softening influence.

Our Home Is This Country

Rita Joe

The dearly loved Cape Breton poet, Rita Joe (1932-2007), was informally known as the Poet Laureate of the Mi'kmaq people. She had ten children and said that all she wanted to be was a housewife. She was that, along with being a mother and the author of half a dozen poetry anthologies, the last of which was, We Are All Dreamers *(1999). Rita Joe started writing poetry at age thirty to challenge images of Aboriginal people taught to her children. "You'll always find beauty wherever you look for it."*

Our home is this country
across the windswept hills
with snow on fields.
The cold air.
I like to think of our native life,
curious, free;
and look at the stars
sending icy messages.
My eyes see the cold face of the moon
cast his net over the bay.
It seems
we are like the moon—
born,
grow slowly,
then fade away, to reappear again
in a never-ending cycle.
Our lives go on
until we are old and wise,
then end.
We are no more,
except we leave
a heritage that never dies.

The Past

Kath Walker

The renowned poet, Kath Walker (1920-1993), was Australia's Rosa Parks. Born on North Stradbroke Island, off the Queensland coast, she started working at age 13 as a maid for two shillings, sixpence a month; three years later she was thwarted in her desire to become an nurse because she was an Aborigine. She was an ardent crusader for Aboriginal rights, working tirelessly for full citizenship of Aboriginal people (1967). Her passionate heart and precise pen gave voice to a whole generation of Aboriginal people.

Let no one say the past is dead.
The past is all about us and within.
Haunted by tribal memories, I know
This little now, this accidental present
Is not the all of me, whose long making
Is so much of the past.

Tonight here in suburbia as I sit
In an easy chair before an electric heater,
Warmed by the red glow. I fall into dream:

I am away
At the camp fire in the bush, among,
My own people, sitting on the ground,
No walls around me,
The stars over me,
The tall surrounding trees that stir the wind
Making their own music,
Soft cries of the night coming to us, there
Where we are one with all Nature's lives
Known and unknown,
In scenes where we belong but have now forsaken.
Deep chair and electric radiator
Are but since yesterday,

But a thousand camp fires in the forest
Are in my blood.
Let none tell us the past is wholly gone.
Now is so small a part in time, so small a part
Of all the race years that have mounded me.

The Holy One Has Made All Things

Sirach 43

Paraphrase by Anne Rowthorn

The book of Sirach (also called Ecclesiasticus) is included in the Apocrypha, which consists of biblical books received by the early church as part of the Greek version of the Old Testament, but not included in the Hebrew Bible. This selection presents a sweeping, poetic, compelling image of the all-powerful God who created the sun, moon, stars, fire, water, lightening, clouds, as well as all manner of plants, animals, fish, and people. The Great God who created it all also upholds and sustains the universe.

The pride of the higher realms is the clear vault of the sky, as glorious to behold as the sight of the heavens. The sun, when it appears, proclaims as it rises what a marvelous instrument it is, the work of the Most High. At noon it parches the land, and who can withstand its burning heat It breaths out fiery vapors. Great is the God who made it.

It is the moon that marks the changing seasons, governing the times, their everlasting sign. From the moon comes the sign of festal days, a light that wanes when it completes its course. The new moon renews itself. How marvelous it is in this change, a beacon to the hosts on high, shining in the vault of the heavens.

The glory of the stars is the beauty of heaven, a glittering array in the heights of Heaven. On the orders of the Holy One they stand in their appointed places; they never relax in their watches.

Look at the rainbow, and praise God who made it; it is exceedingly beautiful in its brightness. It encircles the sky with its glorious arc; the hands of the Most High have stretched it out.

The Holy One sends the driving snow and speeds the lightening. God's storehouses are opened and the clouds fly out like birds. In Majesty God gives the clouds their strength and the hailstones are broken in pieces. God's voice, like a thunder clap, rebukes the earth. When the Holy One appears, the mountains shake. At God's will the south wind blows; so do the storms from the north and the whirlwinds.

The Holy One scatters the snow like birds flying down and its descent is like locusts alighting. The eye is dazzled by the beauty of its whiteness and the mind is amazed as it falls. God pours frost over the earth like salt and icicles form like pointed thorns. The cold north wind blows and ice freezes on the water. It settles on every pool of water and the water puts it on like a breastplate.

God consumes the mountains and burns up the wilderness. God withers the tender grass like fire. A mist quickly heals all things; the falling dew gives refreshment from the heat.

By divine plan the Most High stilled the deep and planted islands in it. In it are strange and marvelous creatures, all kinds of living things and the huge whales of the sea.

Because of the great God of all creation, all things hold together. Awesome is the Holy One and very great. Marvelous is the power of God who has made all things.

You Spread Out the Heavens

Psalm 104

Paraphrase by Anne Rowthorn

"O God, You Spread Out the Heavens" is a paraphrase of Psalm 104 in praise of God the Creator of all. Notice that the psalmist is writing about a God who is creating right now—not a remote, past, or passive deity but a God of the present who is currently creating and sustaining the universe. The creation of the world was not a once and for all occurrence; creation continues the divine project of creativity—right now and to eternity.

O God, you spread out the heavens like a tent.
    You lay the beams of your chambers in the waters above.
    You make the clouds your chariot.
    You ride on the wings of the wind.

You make the winds your messengers,
    and the flames of fire your couriers.
You have set the earth on its foundations
    so that it shall never be moved.
    You covered it with the deep as with a cloak.
    The waters stood higher than the mountains.

At your rebuke they fled;
    at the voice of your thunder they hastened away.
    They went up into the hills and down to the valleys below,
    to the places you appointed for them.

You set the limits that they should not pass
    so that they shall not cover the earth again.

You make springs gush forth from the valleys, they flow between the hills.

All the beasts of the field drink their fill from them,
and the wild asses quench their thirst.
Beside them the birds of the air make their nests
and sing melodies among the branches.

You water your mountains from your dwelling place on high.
The earth is satisfied by the fruit of your work.

You make grass grow for the flocks and herds
and plants for the people's use
that they may bring forth food from the earth
and wine to gladden their spirits,
oil to make their faces shine
and bread to strengthen their hearts.

Your trees are full of sap, the cedars of Lebanon that you planted
in which the birds build their nests and the stork makes its home.

The high hills are a refuge for the mountain goats,
and the stony cliffs for the rock conies.

You appointed the moon to mark the seasons
and the sun knows the time of its setting.
You make darkness and it is night
when the wild beasts of the forest prowl.
The lions roar after their prey, seeking their food from God.
When the sun rises in the morning
they slip away and lie down in their dens.

People go out to their work
and they labor until evening comes and night is at hand.

O Holy God, how manifold are your works;
in wisdom you have made them all.
The earth is full of your creatures.

Yonder is the great and wide sea
    with its living things too numerous to count,
    creatures both small and great.
    There move the ships and there swims the Leviathan*
    that your formed.

All the creatures of the earth look to you
    to give them their food in due season.
    You give it to them and they gather it up.
    You open your hand and they are filled with good things.

When you hide your face they are terrified.
    When you take their breath away they die and return to the dust.

You send forth your spirit and they are created
    and so you renew the face of the earth.

May the glory of the Holy God endure forever;
    may the Sovereign of heaven and earth rejoice in all his works.
God looks on the earth and it trembles, touches the mountains they smoke.

Let us sing to God as long as we live.
    Let us sing the Holy One's praise as long as we have breath.

*Leviathan: A sea monster, perhaps a whale.

Heaven and Earth Abide

Selected Readings from Tao Teh Ching

Lao-Tzu

Tao Te Ching *("The Way") the 2500 year old treasury of wisdom which originated in China, has maintained its appeal throughout all ages and cultures because in very simple and direct terms it speaks eternal truths to those who seek* The Way *in all its fullness. The core teaching of the* Tao Te Ching *is that there is an all-suffusing harmony running throughout creation, an orderly interaction of all life and that the goal of each human being is to put one's self in accord with the Tao and thus live in peace and harmony in the world.*

Heaven and earth abide.
By not living for themselves,
they live forever.

True goodness is like water.
Water gives life to ten thousand things
but does not compete with them.

Keep to simplicity,
Grasp the primal,
Reduce the self,
and curb desire.

Twist and get whole.
Bend and get straight.
Be empty and get filled.
Be worn and get renewed.
Have little; get much.

The universe has four greats:
Humanity,
Earth,
Heaven, and the
Tao.
Humanity follows the earth,
Earth follows heaven,
Heaven follows the *Tao*,
The *Tao* follows itself.

The world is a sacred vessel
Not to be acted upon.
Whoever acts upon it
    destroys it.
Whoever grasps it
    loses it.

Hold to the great *Tao*
    and all beneath heaven will follow.

When the *Tao* is lost,
there is no virtue.
When virtue is lost,
there is no humanness.
When humanness is lost,
there is no morality.
When morality is lost,
there is only ceremony
and the beginning of confusion and folly.

Therefore, the wise person holds to:
The solid,
rather than the shell;
The fruit rather than the blossom.
S/he avoids the outward,
and holds to the inward.

The bright way looks dark.
The forward way look behind.
The smooth way looks rough.
High virtue looks low.

Beneath heaven,
The more laws and prohibitions there are,
the poorer the people become.
The sharper the country's weapons,
the greater its confusion.
The cleverer the people become,
the more deceit takes place.

A journey of a thousand miles
starts where your feet are right now.

When people do not fear force,
greater force is on the way.

Nothing beneath heaven
is softer and weaker than water.
The weak overcomes the strong,
the soft overcomes the hard.

The more s/he gives,
the more s/he receives.
The way of Heaven is to benefit
but not to harm.
They way of the sage is
to work in concert with heaven,
and not to compete.

V

The Solace of Nature

Everybody needs beauty as well as bread, places to play in and pray in, where Nature may heal and cheer and give strength to body and soul.

—John Muir,
The Yosemite

My Cathedral

Henry Wadsworth Longfellow

The beloved New England poet, Henry Wadsworth Longfellow (1807-1882), reminds us that all the great cathedrals of the world are no more effective than cathedrals of the vast outdoors—the stately pines—in bridging seen and unseen, matter and spirit, person and God—and symbolizing the mystical union of all created beings. Amid the sights and sounds and winds of nature, we learn "worship without words."

Like two cathedral towers these stately pines
Uplift their fretted summits tipped with cones;
the arch beneath them is not built with stones,
Not art but nature traced these lovely lines,

And carved this graceful arabesque of vines;
No organ but the wind here sighs and moans,
No sepulcher conceals a martyr's bones,
No marble bishop on his tomb reclines.

Enter! the pavement, carpeted with leaves,
Gives back a softened echo to thy tread!
Listen! the choir is singing; all the birds,

In leafy galleries beneath the eaves,
Are singing! listen ere the sound be fled
And learn there may be worship without words.

Oh Earth, Wait for Me

Pablo Neruda

The Chilean poet, diplomat and politician, Pablo Neruda (1904-1973), is considered one of the most original and prolific poets to write in the Spanish language in the twentieth-century. His talent gained him the Nobel Prize for Literature in 1971. As much a man of compassion as a writer, this precocious son of a railway worker was an ardent lover of life and a champion of the rights of the oppressed and downtrodden.

Return me, oh sun,
to my wild destiny,
rain of the ancient wood,
bring me back the aroma and the swords
that fall from the sky,
the solitary peace of pasture and rock,
the damp at the river margins,
the smell of the larch tree,
the wind alive like a heart
beating in the crowded restlessness
of the towering araucaria.

Earth, give me back your pure gifts,
the towers of silence which rose
from the solemnity of their roots.
I want to go back to being what I have not been,
and learn to go back from such deeps
that amongst all natural things
I could live or not live; it does not matter
to be one stone more, the dark stone,
the pure stone which the river bears away.

Nature

Ralph Waldo Emerson

Ralph Waldo Emerson, one of New England's leading transcendentalist writer/philosophers of the nineteenth century, wrote "Nature" in 1833. Disappointed in the development of his professional life and following the deaths of one of his brothers and his frail and lovely wife of a year, Ellen, he sought the solace of nature for the healing of his grief. For Emerson, to find comfort for life's hurts and disappointments, to know oneself, to know God, to know genuine beauty, to be in touch with the source of the universe, solitude in the natural world was essential.

If one would be alone, let him look at the stars. The rays that come from those heavenly worlds will separate him and what he touches. One might think the atmosphere was made transparent with this design, to give to humanity, in the heavenly bodies, the perpetual presence of the sublime. Seen in the streets of cities, how great they are! If the stars should appear one night in a thousand years, how would people believe and adore; and preserve for many generations the remembrance of the city of God which has been shown! But every night come out these envoys of beauty, and light the universe with their admonishing smile.

The stars awaken a certain reverence, because though always present, they are inaccessible; but all natural objects make a kindred impression, when the mind is open to their influence. Nature never wears a mean appearance. Neither does the wise one exhort her secret, and lose her curiosity by finding all her perfection. Nature never becomes a toy to a wise spirit. The flowers, the animals, the mountains, reflected the wisdom of her best hour, as much as they delighted the simplicity of her childhood.

When we speak of nature in this manner, we have a distinct but most poetical sense in the mind. We mean the integrity of impression made by manifold natural objects. It is this which distinguishes the stick of timber of the wood-cutter from the tree of the poet. The charming landscape which I saw this morning is made up of some twenty or thirty farms. Miller owns this field, Locke that and Manning the woodland beyond. But none of them owns the landscape. There is a property in the horizon which no man has but he whose eye can integrate all the parts. This is the best part of these men's farms, yet to this their warranty deeds give no title.

To speak truthfully, few adult persons can see nature. Most persons do not see the sun. At least they have a superficial seeing. The sun illuminates only the eye of the adult, but shines into the eye and the heart of the child. The lover of nature is the one whose inward and outward senses are still truly adjusted to each other; who has retained the spirit of infancy even into the era of adulthood. Such a person's intercourse with heaven and earth becomes part of her daily food. In the presence of nature a wild delight runs through the person, in spite of real sorrows. Nature says—this is my creature, with all his impertinent griefs, he shall be glad with me. Not the sun or the summer alone, but every hour and season yields its tribute of delight; for every hour and change corresponds to and authorizes a different state of the mind, from breathless noon to grimmest midnight.

Nature is a setting that fits equally well a comic or one in mourning. In good health, the air is a cordial, full of incredible virtue. Crossing a bare common, in snow puddles, at twilight, under a clouded sky, without having in my thoughts any occurrence of special good fortune, I have enjoyed perfect exhilaration. I am glad to the brink of fear. In the woods too, a woman casts off her years, as the snake its skin, and at what period so ever of life is always a child. In the woods is perpetual youth.

Within these plantations of God, a decorum and sanctity reign, a perennial festival is dressed, and the guest sees not how he should tire of them in a thousand years. In the woods we return to reason and faith. There I feel that nothing can befall me in life—no disgrace, no calamity which nature cannot repair. Standing on bare ground—my head bathed by the blithe air and uplifted into infinite space—all mean egoism vanishes. I become a transparent eyeball. I am nothing. I see all. The currents of the Universal Being circulate through me. I am part and parcel of God. The name of the dearest friend sounds foreign and accidental. I am the lover of uncontained and immortal beauty. In the wilderness I find something more dear and connate than in the streets or villages. In the tranquil landscape, and especially in the distant line of the horizon, one beholds something beautiful.

The greatest delight which the fields and woods minister is the suggestion of a relationship between human beings and the natural world. I am not alone and unacknowledged. The trees and plants nod to me and I to them. The waving of the boughs in the storm is new to me and old. It takes me by surprise, and yet is not unknown. Its effect is like that of a higher thought or a better emotion coming over me, when I deemed I was thinking justly or doing right. Yet it is certain that the power to produce this delight does not reside in nature alone, nor in humanity by itself, but in a harmony of both. . . . Nature always wears the colors of the spirit.

The Peace of Wild Things

Wendell Berry

Wendell Berry (b. 1934) is a Kentucky farmer, novelist, poet, and essayist whose works are an extended conversation about sustainable agriculture, living in harmony with creation and a reverence for life. He alternates between dark moments and hopefulness. He said, "We have reached a point at which we must either consciously desire and choose and determine the future of the earth or submit to such an involvement in our destructiveness that the earth, and ourselves with it, must certainly be destroyed." He is renewed when he rests beside a pond contemplating the wood drake and the great heron "who do not tax their lives with forethought or grief."

When despair for the world grows in me
and I wake in the night at the least sound
in fear of what my life and my children's lives may be,
I go and lie down where the wood drake
rests in his beauty on the water, and the great heron feeds.
I come into the peace of wild things
who do not tax their lives with forethought
of grief. I come into the presence of still water.
And I feel above me the great day-blind stars
waiting with their light. For a time
I rest in the grace of the world, and am free.

To the Aurora Borealis

Christopher Pearse Cranch

Christopher Pearse Cranch, a transcendental landscape painter of the Hudson River School and a poet, saw the painting of a landscape or the interpreting it in poetry as a form of religious expression. He covered himself with nature—living in it, breathing in its aromas, feeling its power and caress. "I expand and live in the warm day like corn and melons."

Arctic fount of holiest light,
Springing through the winter night,
Spreading far behind yon hill,
When the earth lies dark and still,
Rippling o'er the stars, as streams
O'er pebbled beds in sunny gleams;
O for names, thou vision fair,
To express thy splendors rare!

Blush upon the cheek of night,
Posthumous, unearthly light,
Dream of the deep sunken sun,
Beautiful, sleep-walking one,
Sister of the moonlight pale,
Star-obscuring meteor veil,
Spread by heaven's watching vestals;
Sender of the gleamy crystals
Darting on their arrowy course

From their glittering polar source,
Upward where the air doth freeze
Round the sister Pleiades;—

Beautiful and rare Aurora,
In the heavens thou art their Flora,
Night-blooming Cereus of the sky,
Rose of amaranthine dye,
Hyacinth of purple light,
Or their Lily clad in white!
Who can name thy wondrous essence,
Thou electric phosphorescence?
Lonely apparition fire!
Seeker of the starry choir!
Restless roamer of the sky,
Who hath won thy mystery?
Mortal science hath not ran
With thee through the Empyrean,
Where the constellations cluster
Flower-like on thy branching luster.

After all the glare and toil,
And the daylight's fretful coil,
Thou dost come so milt and still,
Hearts with love and peace to fill;
As when after revelry
With a talking company,
Where the blaze of many lights
Fell on fools and parasites,
One by one the guests have gone,
And we find ourselves alone;
Only one sweet maiden near,
With a sweet voice low and clear,
Whispering music in our ear,—
So thou talkest to the earth
After daylight's weary mirth.
Is not human fantasy,
Wild Aurora, likest thee,
Blossoming in nightly dreams,

Like thy shifting meteor-gleams?
But a better type thou art
Of the strivings of the heart,
Reaching upward from the earth
To the SOUL that gave it birth.
When the noiseless beck of night
Summons out the inner light
That hath hid its purer ray
Through the lapses of the day—
Then like thee, thou Northern Morn,
Instincts which we deemed unborn,
Gushing from their hidden source
Mount upon their heavenward course
And the spirit seeks to be
Filled with God's eternity.

I Dwell in the Green Mountain

Li Po

Li Po (701-762) is regarded as the greatest poet of the Chinese T'ang Dynasty. He left his home in Szechwan about 720 and for twenty years wandered from place to place only occasionally working. For awhile he was a court poet at the provincial capital of Ch'ang-an, but he preferred his carefree nomadic life.

You ask me why I dwell in the green mountain;
I smile and make no reply for my heart is free to care.
As the peach blossom flows down the stream and is gone
    into the unknown,
I have a world apart that is among no one.

Walden

Henry David Thoreau

If Ralph Waldo Emerson was the most distinguished spirit of the Transcendentalist Movement, Henry David Thoreau (1817-1862), was the movement's most ardent practitioner. Thoreau took up residence at Walden Pond July 4, 1845. For two years he lived on a tract of land belonging to Emerson, his friend and (in the beginning) mentor. His idea was to strip the life down to its barest essentials and there discover the fundamental laws of nature in their archetypal simplicity.

When I wrote the following pages, I lived alone in the woods a mile from any neighbor, in a house which I had built myself, on the shores of Walden Pond, in Concord, Massachusetts, and earned my living by the labor of my hands only. . . .

We may imagine a time when, in the infancy of the human race, some enterprising mortal crept into a hollow in a rock for shelter. Every child begins the world again, to some extent, and loves to stay out doors, even in wet and cold. It plays house as well as horse, having an instinct for it. Who does not remember when young looking at shelving rocks, or any approach to a cave? It was the natural yearning of that portion of our most primitive ancestor which still survived in us. From the cave we have advanced to roofs of palm leaves, of bark and bough, of linen woven and stretched, of grass and straw, of boards and shingles, of stones and tiles. At last we know not what it is to live in the open air, and our lives are domestic in more senses than we think. From the hearth to the field is a great distance. It would be well perhaps if we were to spend more of our days and nights without any obstruction between us and the celestial bodies, if the poet did not speak so much from under a roof, or the saint dwell there so long. Birds do not sing in caves, nor do doves cherish their innocence in dovecotes. . . .

We must learn to reawaken and keep ourselves awake, not by mechanical aids, but by an infinite expectation of the dawn, which does not forsake us in our soundest sleep. . . .

I went to the woods because I wished to live deliberately, to front only the essential facts of life, and see if I could not learn what it had to teach, and not, when I came to die, discover that I had not lived. I wanted to live deep and suck all the marrow out of life. . . .

Time is but a stream I go a-fishing in. I drink at it; but while I drink I see the sandy bottom and detect how shallow it is. Its thin current slides away, but eternity remains. I would drink deeper. . . .

Walk in search of the springs of life. . . . When we walk, we naturally go to the fields and woods. What would become of us if we walked only in a garden or a mall? . . .

The cutting down of a forest and of all large trees simply deforms the landscape, and makes it more and more tame and cheap. . . . People should burn the fences and let the forest stand! . . .

I believe in the forest, and in the meadow, and in the night in which the corn grows. . . . The most alive is the wildest. . . . Hope and the future for me are not in lawns and cultivated fields, not in towns and cities, but in the impervious and quaking swamps. . . . A town is saved, not more by the righteous men in it than by the woods and swamps that surround it. . . . A township where one primitive forest waves above while another primitive forest rots below—such a town is fitted to raise not only corn and potatoes, but poets and philosophers for the coming ages. . . .

Give me the ocean, the desert or the wilderness. In the desert, pure air and solitude compensate for want of moisture and fertility. . . . When I would recreate myself, I seek the darkest wood, the thickest and most interminable. I enter a swamp as a sacred place—a *sanctum sanctorum* (the Holy of Holies). Here is the strength and marrow of nature. . . .

In wilderness is the preservation of the world. . . .

Painter in the Woods

Christopher Pearse Cranch

The poet and landscape painter of the Hudson River School, Christopher Pearse Cranch (1813-1892) illustrates the power of just one beautiful selection of ecological writing. Having graduated from the Harvard Divinity School, Cranch was headed towards his professional life as a Unitarian minister when he read Ralph Waldo Emerson's essay, "Nature." It was a transforming experience and from that moment on, Cranch only wanted to be in the woods. "If art could lead people to God, then artists could replace preachers," he reasoned. So the forest became Cranch's pulpit and he spent the rest of his life painting it and writing about it.

I would go back to the woods or, rather
up to the mountains into the regions of wilder scenery
where the great hemlocks and black birches tower above one another
in the wild centennial garden;
where by the side of the narrow path, the stream brawls and gurgles
and plunges over the rocks, or under immense logs
that have fallen across, some of them old and moss-covered,
others freshly splintered by some late storm. . . .

Or I would still climb upward,
till I stand on the mountain top,
and see the vast, cloud-like, misty landscape below me,
as if the world were all mapped out there;
woods beyond woods, fields beyond fields . . .
and the highest mountains of neighboring states dwarfed by our position.
Higher I cannot go, unless I take a balloon and float among those piles of clouds.
But this I desire not; for the common things of Mother Earth content me;
and I descend cheerful and exhilarated into the valley once more.

The Stars, the Snow, the Fire

John Haines

Nature writing does not get any better than John Haines's recollection of his years in Alaska when he homesteaded from 1954 to 1969 at Mile 68, Richardson Highway, southeast of Fairbanks. Haines lived off the plenty of the land and rivers; he built a cabin and various hunting camps. This selection is a partial account of his three days' journey to one of the camps and his reflections on the ice, the snow, the fire.

In this wilderness life I have found a way to touch the world once more. One way. To live the life that is here to be lived, as nearly as I can without that other—clock hands, hours, and wages. I relive each day the ancient expectation of the hunt—the setting out, and the trail at dawn. What will we find today?

I leave my mankindness behind me for a while and become part tree, a creature of the snow. It is a long way back, and mostly in the shadow. I see a little there, not much, but what I see will never be destroyed.

I may not always be here in these woods. The trails I have made will last a long time; this cabin will stand at least twenty years before it falls. I can imagine a greater silence, a deeper shadow where I am standing, but what I have loved will always be here. Night and day passes. Evening, another pot of stew. . . . The weather holding steady, still twenty-nine below. . . . .

I take my pack and, stick in hand, set off up the trail toward Glacier Creek. . . . . In late afternoon I walked the last mile home along the Tanana, through the woods on a steep hillside. . . . The sun was gone, the light on the river, on the ice, a steely grey. Clouds were building a heavy darkness in the west. Sounds came to me along the river: water running somewhere out on the ice, a dog barking. . . .

I sit here now, the long day over and the pack gone from my shoulders at last. My heavy clothing removed, moccasins hung up to dry, gloves and mittens drying on the rack above the stove. Half-sleepy, warmed by the fire, while Jo makes supper and we talk. . . .

I am happy deep inside. Not the mind-tiredness of too much thought, of thoughts that pursue each other endlessly in that forest of nerves, anxiety, and fear. But the stretching kind of tiredness, the ease and satisfaction of time well spent, and of the deep self renewed.

VI

Air, Sky, and Stars

On the sea of heaven the clouds arise,
and the moon's ship is seen sailing
to hide in the forest of stars.

—Author unknown
Japanese poem from the seventh century

The Is Sky in Me

Jackson Zinn-Rowthorn

Jackson Zinn-Rowthorn is an eleven-year-old award-winning poet who has a strong affinity with the natural world. This poem, one of 1200 submitted, was selected for inclusion in the publication, Connecticut Student Writers. *In introducing it, Jackson said, "My poem compares my personality and spirit with the boundless sky."*

In me resides a cloud.
It transports me lavishly and tranquilly
from barren desert to metropolis.
It cultivates my interest
in following the ways of life,
in comprehending the sights I witness,
and in living life in
a steady, carefree tempo
that beats only when I keep this cloud in my grasp.
And I will
because it was a gift from the Sky,
and the Sky will not take it back.

In me resides the sun.
Shining within
like a gyroscope
destined to assist
and shed its rays luminously on any situation.
Its heat warms me,

either too much
or exactly accurately,
depending on whether
I honor this light of the universe.
And I will
because it is a gift from the Sky,
and the Sky will not take it back.

In me reside the stars,
shimmering orbs of radiance,
whose illumination seems imperial and arrogant.
They quiver,
appear and disappear,
depending upon the clarity of the night.
Petrified objects lighting the darkness,
the diminutive stars
reveal the vastness of the universe
if I open my eyes to their luminosity.
And I will
because they are a gift from the Sky,
and the Sky will not take them back.

In me reside creatures of the air,
some regal, others cruel,
whose beaks and wings seem alien
to the unknowing animals of the ground.
For us, we have land;
the fish and mammals of the water have the sea;
the majestic birds have air,
air that covers every land and the unending horizons of the sea.
I want to keep these birds safe.
And I will,
for they were a gift from the Sky,
and the Sky will not take them back.

In me resides the wind,
wind that moves the clouds,
holds the birds in their flight
and moderates the sun's relentless rays.
The wind is the leader.
It would only halt if its work were through
but its work is never through.
From a whiff of breeze on a languid summer's day to a mighty cyclone,
the wind is always with us.
I can't depart from the wind.
And I won't,
because it is a gift from the Sky,
and the Sky will not take it back.

The Sky is in me,
its howling wind my vitality,
its creatures my personality,
its stars my questing,
its sun, my vision,
its clouds my eagerness—
all given to me by the Sky,
and the Sky will not take them back.

In California

Denise Levertov

The eloquent British-born American poet, Denise Levertov (1923-1997), said that "... it has become ever clearer to all thinking people that although we humans are a part of nature ourselves, we have become, in multifarious ways, an increasingly destructive element within it, shaking and breaking the 'great web'—perhaps irremediably."

Morning

Pale, then enkindled,
Light
Advancing,
Emblazoning
Summits of palm and pine,

The dew
lingering,
scripture of
scintillas.

Soon the roar
of mowers
cropping the already short
grass of lawns,

men with long-nozzled
cylinders of pesticide
poking at weeds,
at moss in cracks of cement,

and louder roar
of helicopters off to spray
vineyards where braceros try
to hold their breath,

and in the distance, bulldozers, excavators,
babel of destructive construction.

Banded by deep
Oakshadow, airy
shadow of eucalyptus,

miner's lettuce,
tender, untasted,
and other grass, unmown,
luxuriant,
no green more brilliant.

Fragile paradise.

Evening

At day's end the whole sky,
vast, unstinting, flooded with transparent
mauve,
tint of wisteria,
cloudless
over the malls, the industrial parks
the homes with the lights going on,
the homeless arranging their bundles.

Late January

Who can utter
the poignance of all that is constantly
threatened, invaded, expended

and constantly
nevertheless
persists in beauty,

tranquil as this young moon
just risen and slowly
drinking light
from the vanishing sun.

Who can utter
the praise of such generosity
or the shame?

Matariki is Appearing in the Sky

Māori Oral Tradition

Author Unknown

The Pleiades are known by Māoris as Matariki. In the Southern Hemisphere the constellation rises in May and June, marking the beginning of their new year. Its arrival announces the time when all agreements became null and void and new ones made. The Pleiades numbers hundreds of stars; with the naked eye, the Māori saw seven stars, thus its popular name of the Seven Sisters.

Look away here, Matariki is appearing in the sky.
The seven stars of the new year,
Twinkling there giving their tidings
That make me rejoice. . . .

High Country Weather

James K. Baxter

James K. Baxter (1926-1972) is considered by some as New Zealand's greatest poet. He wrote his first poem at age seven; by the time he was twenty he'd written another thousand. He published his first volume at seventeen. His impatience with institutions of conformity saw him quit college and work at a variety of jobs—farm laborer, factory worker, hospital orderly, postman. He fought alcoholism all his life, and his restless spirituality led him to convert to Roman Catholicism, although he was ever a thorn in the side of the orthodox believer. Religion, love, myth, and the majestic New Zealand landscape were central poetic themes, but he placed people above all. At the end of his life wrote: "Where does one's hope lie? Not, I think, in the mental or material engines of technology. My own hope lies in the hearts of people . . ."

Alone we are born
　　And die alone;
Yet see the red-gold cirrus
　　Over snow-mountain shine.

Upon the upland road
　　Ride easy, stranger:
Surrender to the sky
　　Your heart of anger.

Brother Air

Helder Camara

Perhaps we don't think very much about the air around us that supports all life on this planet, but Helder Camara compares air to our loving Creator God who never leaves us from our first breath to our last sigh.

Have you noticed
How we humans
For all our civilization
Transform you,
The guarantor of life
Into a spreader of poisons?
Have you noticed
How we humans,
Gifted with intelligence and reason,
Are wounding nature
And preparing disasters
For ourselves
With our own hands?

How do you feel
When a thousand sounds,
Words and music,
Threats and songs of love,
Pass through you each instant?
How marvelous it would be
If everything you carried
Were at the service
Of peace and goodness.

Do you feel the difference
Between the flight of a bird
And the throb of an aircraft?
Do you see the spaceships
Shooting by?
Do you go with them?
In those far reaches
Is there still need of you?

No doubt you have knowledge
You cannot reveal . . .
No doubt you know well
The things beyond earth,
And always and everywhere
You feel in a wonderful way
The presence of your
Creator God.

Do you know that
You give us
Of all images
One most close to God?

We live
Inside God
Everywhere
At all times,
Just as we live
Inside you.

And just as we
Think rarely of you
By day and still
Less at night,
So do we rarely

Think of our God.
If we are without you
Even a few seconds,
Life is unbearable!
Only then do we think
Of you.
Our God fades from our thought
Even more, yet God never
Complains of the way
We leave the Holy One alone;
And God never leaves us!
O Air, please teach us
To think of you
And still more, much more,
To think of God,
Our Creator and yours.

A Song of the Pleiades

Pawnee Oral Tradition

Author Unknown

Our forebears looked to the heavens for wisdom and guidance. It is said that a bright star in the East led the people to the place where Jesus was born. Here the poet looks to the constellation, Pleiades, and prays that, like the twins of the night sky, we too may be united.

Look as they rise, rise
Over the line where sky meets the earth;
Pleiades!
Lo! They ascending, come to guide us,
Leading us safely, keeping us one;
Pleiades,
Teach us to be, like you,
United.

The Song of the Stars

Algonquin Oral Tradition

Author Unknown

It has been said that every being in the universe has a voice. In this beautiful poem we are introduced to the Algonquin idea that the light of the night sky is none other than the melody of the stars.

We are the stars which sing,
We sing with our light;
We are the birds of fire,
We fly over the sky.
Our light is a voice;
We make a road for spirits,
For the spirits to pass over.
Among us are three hunters
Who chase a bear;
There never was a time
When they were not hunting.
We look down on the mountains.
This is the Song of the Stars.

Earth's Embroidery

Solomon Ibn Gabriol

Solomon Ibn Gabriol (1021-1058) was one of the most talented and versatile poet-philosophers of the Golden Age of Hebrew Literature (mid-tenth century to the end of the fifteenth century). Born in Cordova and raised in Malaga, Gabriol was orphaned at an early age. He made philosophy, the natural world, and solitude his only friends and companions.

With the ink of its showers and its rains,
with the quill of its lightening,
with the hand of its clouds,
winter wrote a letter upon the garden,
    in purple and blue.
No artist could ever conceive the like of that.
And this is how the earth,
    grown jealous of the sky,
    embroidered stars in the folds
    of the flower beds.

VII

The Sun Descends Into Night

Nighttime . . . The soft darkness penetrates the soul. The sky darkens and the earth and sky merge under the immensity of the starry heavens. Night is the time of poetry. It is the time of deep dreams.

—Erazim Kohák,

Between the Embers and the Stars

Night, Do you Know?

La Bedbedin

The people of the Republic of the Marshall Islands have a rich oral tradition of chants, songs, and legends. To this day, most of it remains oral. The stories of La Bedbedin, whose anglicized name is "Man This Reef," were recorded and translated by Gerald Knight, a Peace Corps volunteer in the Marshall Islands, in the 1970s. La Bedbedin, a natural poet, was 78 years old at the time. This chant would have been intoned by sailors navigating at night through the hundreds of miles of sea.

Night to feel in darkness for those we know.
Night to feel your way and test—do you know?
Night of sleeplessness to show
you are captain of the sea.
Are you captain of the sea?
Night of blackness now—
thick night of storm.
Those safe on land wake now to morn.
Night of strong wind and rain and kior cloud.
Afraid now of ocean or following proud?
Night of blackness now—
thick night of storm.
Those safe on land
wake now to morn.

No Ordinary Sun

Hone Tuwhare

The volume containing this poem bearing the same name, No Ordinary Sun, *became one of the most widely read individual poetry collections in New Zealand history. Its author, Māori poet Hone Tuwhare (1922-2008), was born in Kaikohe, on the North Island but spent most of his childhood in Auckland. He trained as a boilermaker and when* No Ordinary Sun *was published in 1964, he was a tradesman working at a hydro-electric project. The volume brought Tuwhare widespread fame and established his place in New Zealand literary tradition. The poem's warning is even more critical today than ever.*

Tree let your arms fall:
raise them not sharply in supplication
to the bright enhaloed cloud.
Let your arms lack toughness and
resilience for this is no mere axe
to blunt nor fire to smother.

Your sap shall not rise again
to the moon's pull.
No more incline a deferential head
to the wind's talk, or stir
to the tickle of coursing rain.

Your former shagginess shall not be
wreathed with the delightful flight
of birds nor shield
nor cool the ardour of unheeding
lovers from the monstrous sun.

Tree let your naked arms fall
nor extend vain entreaties to the radiant ball.
This is no gallant monsoon's flash,
no dashing trade wind's blast.

The fading green of your magic
emanations shall not make pure again
these polluted skies . . . for this
is no ordinary sun.

O tree
in the shadowless mountains
the white plains and
the drab sea floor
your end at last is written.

Morning Person

Vassar Miller

Poet Laureate of Texas, Vassar Miller (1924-1998) struggled all her life with cerebral palsy which affected both speech and movement, but her poetic voice was clear and strong. Anyone who is an early riser will resonate to the poet's sense that morning is the best time of day.

God, best at making in the morning, tossed
stars and planets, singing and dancing, rolled
Saturn's rings spinning and humming, twirled the earth
so hard it coughed and spat the moon up, brilliant
bubble floating around it for good, stretched holy
Hands till birds in nervous sparks flew forth from
them and beasts—lizards, big and little, apes,
lions, elephants, dogs and cats cavorting,
tumbling over themselves, dizzy with joy when
God made us in the morning too, both man
and woman, leaving Adam no time for
sleep so nimbly was Eve bouncing out of
his side till as night came everything and
everybody, growing tired, declined, sat
down in one soft descending Hallelujah.

The Golden Womb of the Sun

Rig Veda

Interpreted by the Writers Workshop of Calcutta, India

Humankind has a fundamental need to come to terms with its origins. A god, a divine force, an occurrence, sometimes cataclysmic, brought the world into being. Virtually every culture has its creation account. This creation story, "The Golden Womb of the Sun," comes from the most ancient of Hinduism's revealed scriptures, the Rig Veda, *probably composed sometime between 3,000 and 2,000* B.C.E. *The* Rig Veda *is the oldest document of the world's living religions; it is made up of animistic songs and prayers personifying nature and attributing divine personalities to its forces.*

In the beginning was the golden womb of the sun,
Only he and nothing else.
He established the earth and the sky.

Even the brightest gods respect his words.
Breath-giver, life giver,
One half of his shadow is immortality, the other half death.

Mighty ruler,
Lord of the breathing and sleeping world,
King of man and beast.

The snowy mountains declare his glory.
The rivers and the sea declare his glory.
The mountains and the waters are his twin arms.

He made firm the earth and the starry sky,
Earth and the sky ether.
He measured the air in the firmament.

Two armies, sky and earth, tremble,
Clash, or stand firm in his will.
The risen sun looks over his shoulder.

Everywhere are the great waters,
Carrying the golden womb of the sun:
From them came light, the breath of the gods.

He looks on the waters,
Powerful and shining;
Pleased with himself, God above all other gods.

God of the earth,
    protect us;
God of the sky,
    protect us;
God of the great and shining waters,
    protect us.

God above all other gods,
God of the Golden sun, God of all,
    we shall worship you.

Toward the Bosom of the Newly Rising Sun

Tujin Pak

Tujin Pak (1916-1998) was one of Korea's best-known poets. Pak's themes come from the physical world—mountains, trees, the sea, the sun. Read this poem outside in a place of natural beauty when you greet the new day.

Behold the sun. Behold the sun blaze fire as it rises.
Let us walk on the fresh fragrant grass when the sun
rises over the hill. Let us take the dazzling path at dawn
toward the sun.

Be gone, Darkness. Be gone, Darkness that moans
like a beast. Be gone, like beasts, herding onto the cliff.
Onto the cliff, sunlight loaded on your back.

Behold those mountain flowers giving a pungent smell.
Behold those green leaves of trees fluttering as if they dance.
Listen to the melodies of birds, to the song of the waters
that meander through the valleys. The sound that the
whole mountain makes as it wakes again to receive the light.

The grass sound the grass makes on its leaves.
The leaf sound the trees make on their leaves.
The fish sound the minnow-like silver fish make.
As they mill around in schools in the clear water.
The stone sound the stones make as they are tossed down.

The measuring worms on the branches
and the slugs on the bottom.
Cheered, I shout "yahoy ho," baptized in the sun.

Low and faint but withering in unison
rings the songbird of all things green in the mountain.
Of all living things in the mountain.

Mountain, green mountain with leaves of trees fluttering.

When the sun leaps and radiates
My ears open at your fresh sounds;

My eyes brighten at your fresh light.
Blood circulates afresh.

The whole body tingles as if to soar into the air.
I feel light as a bird,
As I walk onto the green morning road,
Walk toward the bosom of the newly rising sun.

The White Sun Has Sunk Beyond the Hills —

Wang Zhihuan

The enormous appeal of Chinese landscape poetry to the western ear—as illustrated by Wang Zhihuan's verse—is that it evokes an intimate expression of personal feeling. There is an immediacy about it which reaches out to touch the core of our being. This effect is achieved through the poet's deep penetration into both the particular and the present. The yellow river is pouring into the sea right now, not yesterday, not tomorrow—but right now.

The white sun has sunk behind the hills.
The yellow river is pouring into the sea.
To see still further into the horizon,
Let us go up one more story!

Night

William Blake

William Blake (1757-1825), a British lyric poet and painter, was one of the best exemplars of the first generation of romantics that included William Wordsworth and Samuel Taylor Coleridge, as well as artists Thomas Gainsborough and J.M.W. Turner. During the second half of the nineteenth century, writers and artists were rediscovering nature which they often personalized and glorified. In "Night," Blake presents a peaceable world watched over by angels who unseen "pour blessing and joy without ceasing."

The sun descending in the west
The evening star does shine,
The birds are silent in their nest
And I must seek for mine.
The moon, like a flower
In heaven's high bower,
With silent delight
Sits and smiles on the night.

Farewell green fields and happy groves
Where flocks have took delight;
Where lambs have nibbled, silent moves
The feet of angels bright;
Unseen they pour their blessing
And joy without ceasing
On each bud and blossom
And each sleeping bosom.

They look in every thoughtless nest
Where birds are covered warm,
They visit caves of every beast
To keep them all from harm.
If they see any weeping
That should have been sleeping,
They pour sleep on their head
And sit down by their bed.

There Is Still Night

Erazim Kohák

As the technologies of our lives have alienated us from the natural world and ourselves, the Czech philosopher, Erazim Kohák invites us to seek the darkness of the forest and the stillness of night and there discover our own true selves in rhythm with the natural world. Solidly grounded in the primordial rhythms of life, we regain our perspective on humankind's place in the world.

There is still night, down where the long-abandoned wagon road disappears amid the new growth beneath the tumbled dam, deep, virgin darkness as humans had known it through millennia, between the glowing embers and the stars. Here the dusk comes softly, gathering beneath the hemlocks and spreading out over the clearing, muting the harsh outlines of the day. There is a time to listen to the stillness of the forest when the failing light signals the end of the day's labor but the gathering darkness does not warrant kindling a lamp. Here time is not of the clock: there is a time of going forth and a time of returning, and there is night, oft, all-embracing, all-reconciling, restoring the soul. On the clear nights of the new moon, the heavens declare the glory of God and the ageless order of the forest fuses with the moral law within. Here a human can dwell with the world, with God and self.

In the global city of our civilization, girded by the high tension of our powerlines, we have abolished the night. There the glare of electric lights extends the unforgiving day far into the night restless with the eerie glow of neon. We walk on asphalt, not on the good earth; we look up at neon, not at the marvel of the starry heavens. Seldom do we have the chance to see virgin darkness, unmarred by electric light, seldom can we recall the ageless rhythm of nature and of the moral law which our bodies and spirits yet echo beneath the heavy layer of forgetting. The world of artifacts and constructs with which we have surrounded ourselves knows neither a law nor a rhythm: in its context, even rising and resting come to seem arbitrary. We ourselves have constructed that world for our dwelling place, replacing rude nature with the artifacts of *techne*, yet increasingly we confess ourselves bewildered strangers within it, alienated into anonymous machinery, and tempted to abolish the conflict between our meaningful humanity and our mechanical life-world by convincing ourselves that we too are but machines.

We stand in danger of losing something crucial—clarity of vision. Surrounded by artifacts and constructs, we tend to lose sight, literally as well as metaphorically, of the rhythm of the day and the night, of the phases of the moon and the change of the seasons, of the life of the cosmos and of our place in it. The vital order of nature and the moral order of humanity remain constant, but they grow overlaid with forgetting.

To recapture the moral sense of life and the world, even the world of artifacts, humans need to bracket it, seeing beyond it to the living world of nature. It takes the virgin darkness to teach us the moral sense of electric light. It takes the beauty of solitude to enable us to grasp the sense of the word spoken over the distance, the crystal-bright gift of pain to teach us the moral sense of penicillin.

VIII

The Rhythm of the Seasons

South of the house, north of the house, everywhere the waters of spring;
I can see only the flocks of gulls that arrive day after day.

—Tu Fu (712-770 C.E.),
A Visitor Has Come

From the Japanese Garden

Ken Arnold

The object of haiku, a poetic art form originating in Japan, is to paint a mental image in the reader's mind in three lines of seventeen syllables. Ken Arnold, a Portland, Oregon poet, playwright, publisher, and shakuhachi player, says that he is increasingly experiencing the world itself as sacred. "I began writing haiku as a way of seeing more clearly the world around me during my recovery from prostate cancer. The form for me is an extension of Zen meditation, articulating the visible, the moment of discovery." Ken's haiku offered here are all based on his experiences in the Portland Japanese Garden.

Rivulets over
the autumn leaves
one sunlit hydrangea

Water striders on
the sundappled pond
not moving

Sunrise on the spiral
of the spider's web
the August Redwood

The Rhythm of the Earth's Seasons

Poetic phrases from a variety of Japanese poets

Translated by Laura Rasplica Rodd and Mary Catherine Henkenius

The poems of "The Rhythm of the Earth's Seasons" are taken from the Kokinshū (A Collection of Poems Ancient and Modern), *the earliest anthology of Japanese poems. It was commissioned by the emperor and compiled sometime around 900 C.E. It was traditional for poets to record their impressions of the seasons as they came and waned.*

Spring

Warm breezes blowing
down the valley slopes melt the
winter's ice at each
crack a foamy wave bubbles
upward springs first showy blossoms.

—Minamoto no Masazumi

On the wings of the
wind I'll send the fragrant scent
of plum blossoms
a summons of spring to guide
that longed for mountain thrush to me.

—Ki no Tomonori

Because I make my
home near the fields and meadows
each and every
morning I hear the song of
the mountain thrush trilling spring.

—Anonymous

Summer

The early days of
summer must already have
passed me unawares—
just now deep in the mountains
the nightingale sang his song.

—Anonymous

By midsummer the
voice of the nightingale will
be well past its prime
oh that I might hear it sing
just once in early season.

—Ise

Tonight as summer
and autumn cross paths on their
journey through the sky
this evening is covered
with a chilly dew.

—Anonymous

Autumn

Flying wing in wing
across the white clouds of the
night sky the wild geese
go their very number
vivid beneath the autumn moon.

—Anonymous

As night deepens it
seems midnight must be near for
only the cries of the
wild geese are heard and the moon
has climbed high in the dark sky.

—Anonymous

The colors of autumn
visible in the thousand
changing hues of the
blowing wind are swirling leaves
tossed about by passing gusts.

—Anonymous

If I knew the road
I would go searching having
offered up multi-hued fallen leaves for prayers
as the twilight approaches.

—Ki no Tsurayuki and
Oshikochi no Mitsune

Winter

As evening deepens
the sleeves of my robe grow cold—
in fair Yoshino
on lovely Mount Yoshino
soft white snow must be falling

—Anonymous

May it continue
to fall forever lovely
white snow bending
the gracefully swaying stalks
of plum grass in my garden.

—Anonymous

When the snow crystals
fall on the sleeping trees and
grasses there bloom wild
flowers that are never seen
on branches or stems in spring.

—Ki no Tsurayuki

At the Year's End

The year's end when snow
blankets all the earth in white
then at last the pines
who know no autumn glory
stand forth in all their splendor.

—Anonymous

"Yesterday, " we say
and "today" we live but still
months and days slip past
as smoothly and as swiftly as
Tomorrow River's waters.

—Harumichi no Tsuraki

Green Leaves, White Water

Selected Haiku from the Works of the Poet Buson

Translated by Robert Hass

Buson (1716-1783) was not only a great poet but also a distinguished painter of his day. He was born near Osaka, the son of a wealthy farmer. When he was twenty he went to Edo (Tokyo) to study poetry and painting, especially the Chinese masters of the T'ang school. Later he wandered through the north country of Japan, retracing Bashō's journeys. Buson's writing is prized for its clarity and sense of the aliveness of things and their presence.

Green leaves,
white water,
the barley yellowing.

The spring sea rising
and falling, rising
and falling all day.

Ploughing the land—
not even a bird singing
in the mountain's shadow.

Not quite dark yet
and the stars shining
above the withered fields.

In the summer rain
the path
has disappeared.

Wild geese returning
on a night when in every rice field
the mood is clouding.

By moonlight
the blossoming plum
is a tree in winter.

Not a leaf stirring;
frightening,
the summer grove.

The end of spring
lingers
in the cherry blossoms.

Spring Song

Robert Browning

"Spring Song" is taken from Robert Browning's well-known poem, "Pippa Passes." Browning (1812-1889), a poet of the Romantic Era, considered himself mainly a botanist, which would explain why so many of his themes were drawn from nature. The change of seasons is a universal poetic theme which transcends culture and time. After the long, cold winters of northern climes, the arrival of spring was particularly welcomed.

The year's at the spring
And day's at the morn;
Morning's at seven;
The hillside's dew-pearled;
The lark's on the wing;
The snail's on the thorn;
God's in his heaven—
All's right with the world.

New Feet Within My Garden Go

Emily Dickinson

Only two of Emily Dickinson's (1830-1886) now famous poems were published during her lifetime. The rest of her 1500 poems were discovered after her death, mostly written on scraps of paper and scattered about in drawers and boxes. By the time she was thirty-five, her world had been circumscribed by her father's house and garden where "New Feet within My Garden Go" was written.

New feet within my garden go—
New fingers stir the sod.
A troubadour upon the elm
Betrays the solitude.

New children play upon the green—
New weary sleep below,
And still the pensive spring returns,
And still the punctual snow.

We Rejoice In this Season of Spring

Edward Hays

The light of the universe enters our hearts and souls as we welcome the new light of spring. The freshness of the spring air refreshes our spirits.

As the earth once again
turns to face the sun
we rejoice in this season of spring.
We give thanks, O God,
that each day grows longer in light
and that the earth has been liberated from
the grip of winter.

Spring

Mary Oliver

The celebrated contemporary poet, Mary Oliver, offers this reflection on a bear in springtime. It begs the question—What is the essence of a bear's life?—and provokes another: What is the essence of ours? Can we love perfectly and wordlessly?

Somewhere
    a black bear
        has just risen from sleep
            and is starting

down the mountain.
    All night
        In the brisk and shallow restlessness
            Of early spring

I think of her,
    Her four black fists
        Flicking the gravel,
            Her tongue

Like a red fire
    touching the grass,
        the cold water.
            There is only one question:

How to love this world.
    I think of her
        rising
            like a black and leafy ledge

to sharpen her claws against
    the silence
        of the trees.
            Whatever else

my life is
    with its poems
        and its music
            and its glass cities,

it is also this dazzling darkness
    coming
        down the mountain,
            breathing and tasting;

all day I think of her—
    her white teeth,
        her wordlessness,
            her perfect love.

In My Grass Hut

Ryōkan

Ryōkan (1758-1831),was influenced by the masters of the ancient Chinese T'ang Dynasty, in which an economy of words carried a profound message. In Ryōkan's spare, well-chosen words, the reader of the following four selections vividly hears and sees what he experienced. He lived alone in a simple hut supporting himself by begging and devoting his time to meditation. His companions on Mount Kugami were the changing seasons, snow, insects, and the poetry of the Chinese masters.

In my grass hut
I wake to hear
showers of hail
rattling over
the grove of bamboo

How pleasant—
in my grass hut
stretching out my legs
listening to the sound
of frogs in mountain paddies.

On leaves of the plantain
growing by the eaves
of my hut
moonlight shines,
the night by now far gone.

Cuckoo Songs

As I cross the summer hills
I see a cuckoo
dart through treetops
beating his wings
and singing.

On green hills
the hue of
the water duck's wing,
a cuckoo lingers
singing in the treetops.

The First Fall Winds

The sadness
of this passing autumn—
who to talk it out with?
a basket of wild spinach picked,
heading home at twilight.

In the autumn meadow
dew that clings
to each clump of grass—
is it the tears of the insects
that cried all night long?

No reason,
yet it makes me sad—
by my door
the first fall winds
rustling through rice stalks.

Autumn wind
day by day
blows colder,
cries of the crickets
each time feebler than before.

The Dark of Winter

Dark of winter, eleventh month,
rain and snow slushing down;
a thousand hills all one color,
ten thousand paths where almost no one goes.
Past wanderings all turned to dreams;
grass gate, its leaves latched tight;
through the night I burn chips of wood,
quietly reading poems written long ago.

Behold the Spring Has Come

Chief Sitting Bull

These words are said to have been spoken by Sitting Bull (1831-1890), the Lakota warrior who was the last Native American chief to surrender to the United States government.

Behold, the spring has come.
The earth has received the embrace of the sun
    and we shall soon see the results of that love.

Every seed has awakened
    and so has all animal life.
It is through this mysterious power
    that we too have our being,
    and we therefore yield to our own neighbors,
    the same right as ourselves to
    inhabit this land.

Ten Thousand Things Respond to Spring Sun

Ou-Yang Hsiu

Ou-Yang Hsiu (1007-1072, Sung Dynasty) was a both a poet and a politician. As a Confucian master, he believed in the practical application of Confucianism to politics. As a poet he exhibits a directness and simplicity combined with great fluency. He was the acknowledged leader of the literary world of his generation.

Spring days are quiet, growing longer.
Fragrant wind enters the heart of the flowers;
Flowering branches at midday bob up and down.
Back and forth the bee picks among the blossoms;
his comb is not yet filled with clear honey.
Spring nights are most beautiful now;
Fallen petals one by one swirl through the air.
Yellow butterflies, nothing else to do,
Fly here and there to help them in their hurry.
Singing birds change their tune from time to time,
New notes skillfully blown from their flutes.
Spider webs are the idlest of all,
Their sunny light dangling a hundred feet.
The Heavenly Craftsman tends to creation's changes;
The ten thousand things respond to spring sun.

The Spring Equinox

Edward Hays

Since the most ancient times, pilgrims of this planet have welcomed the changing of the seasons with rituals and celebrations. In our day may we also be enriched by of the changes that come about through the movements of the earth in her sacred journey around the sun.

As the suns rays strike our planet more directly, the earth responds with newness and freshness. Prehistoric priesthoods set this day apart as sacred, as a feast to celebrate the resurrection of the earth. The sun, radiant and healing, revitalizes the dark and dormant, as days and nights are again of equal length on the day of the equinox. May the external experience of spring prepare each of us for a personal rebirth and resurrection. May it be a pledge sign that life rises out of death.

A true planetary pilgrim experiences this feast not as a spectator but as a concelebrant with the earth and all creation. This day is both holy and magical, filled with hidden spirits and sounds. May our ears, eyes and nose be attentive to the rebirth of green life pushing up through the earth, even if it is still hidden from view. May we feel in our bodies the energy of the sun calling us to newness and life.

The Ancient Ones danced like children to the mystery of new life and sprouting vegetation. They lit great fires to banish the tired, aged spirits of winter and darkness. They built their bonfires to ward off the half-hidden fears that perhaps this time, this year, winter would not leave and they would die in the barren, icy darkness.

With reverence, we let ourselves be touched by this hidden memory as we respond to the tidal-gravitational tug of the planet Earth on this feast of the Spring Equinox. Let us rejoice with all the Web of Life, woven so tightly, as the season of spring begins.

Midsummer's Eve

Diane Ackerman

Diane Ackerman (b. 1948) is a poet, essayist, and naturalist, best known for her book, A Natural History of the Senses. *In reflecting upon her writing at the border lands between human nature and the natural world, Ackerman has said: "We share instincts and emotions with the rest of the natural world. And part of the predicament that we find ourselves in—existentially—is this tragic attempt that we're making to separate ourselves from nature. To exile ourselves from nature is biologically impossible. And yet we pretend that we can do it, as if nature didn't include us somehow. But I also see nature as including everything that is made; the technological wilderness of cities. Nature includes everything."*

Midsummer's Eve, on June 23, falls two days after the summer solstice. Once it was said to be the witches' sabbath, when an evil spell could dishearten the coming harvest. On that night, if a maiden put yarrow sprigs beneath her pillow, she would dream of her future husband. On that night, bathing in a fern seed could make a man invisible, and walking backward with a hazel twig between his knees would lead him to treasure. Summer solstice is just a little Sabbath with the sun. Indeed, summer officially begins with the solstice, from the Latin *solstitium*, "sun standing still." For a few days, the sun rises and sets in almost the same spot on the horizon, a prelude to the longest day of the year, and then the sun begins to crawl south through imperceptibly shorter days, toward a still-unimaginable winter. But for a moment it is early, spine-tingling summer. Jasmine and pine leaden the scents of evening. Spores like manna drill the sky. Pheasant eggs sneak life out of damp sod. Summer disavows any passion stronger than earth's in the sound of rain, in open field, when drizzle breaks into downpour.

Nothing Gold Can Stay

Robert Frost

Although Robert Frost (1874-1963) had variously worked as a farmer, a mill hand, shoemaker, and teacher, the only thing he ever really wanted to do was to write poetry. An enduring poem is one that stays alive because it is rooted in mortal things and immortal emotions. Robert Frost said that a poem that truly satisfies—and "Nothing Gold Can Stay" is an example—will begin with ". . . a lump in the throat, a homesickness or a lovesickness. It is a reaching out toward expression; an effort to find fulfillment, where an emotion has found its voice and the thought has found the words."

Nature's first green is gold,
Her hardest hue to hold.
Her early leaf's a flower;
But only so an hour.
Then leaf subsides to leaf.
So Eden sank to grief,
So dawn goes down to day.
Nothing gold can stay.

The First Snow of the Year

Haiku from four Japanese poets

Translated by R. H. Blyth

It was a universally held belief in Japan that literature came into being at the time the universe was created. R. H. Blyth, the translator of "The First Snow of the Year," who first introduced haiku to English-speaking readers, described haiku as "a record of a moment of emotion in which human nature is somehow linked to all nature."

The first snow of the year,
On the bridge
They are making.

—Bashō

The first snow;
Beyond the sea,
What mountains are they?

—Shiki

There is neither heaven nor earth,
Only snow
Falling incessantly.

—Hashin

Fields and mountains—
The snow has taken them all,
Nothing remains.

—Joso

Snow Is Falling

Boris Pasternak

Boris Pasternak (1890-1960), the great Russian novelist, was first and foremost a poet. His first volume of poetry was published just before World War I. He appended twenty-five poems to his novel, Dr. Zhivago, *published in 1957. Pasternak survived the immense hardships and upheavals of Russian society in the twentieth century. He was discredited by the government, and many of his manuscripts lost and confiscated, yet this humble poet never lost his sense of the wonder of God's creation nor the simple pleasure of watching the snow fall in the depths of a cold Russian winter.*

Snow is falling, snow is falling:
Stretching to the window pane
Pale geraniums gaze out
Where the starflakes blow white rain.

Snow is falling, all's a flurry,
Everything wings off and flies:
Steps down in the shadowed staircase,
Corner where the crossroads rise.

Snow is falling, snow is falling—
Somehow, though, not flakes teem round
But heaven's arch, in ragged furs,
Is descending to the ground.

Looking like an old eccentric,
From the upper landing sly—
Creeping, playing hide-and-seek—
From its attic steals the sky.

Flow of life is not for waiting;
Eyelid's wink, Christmas is here:
Just a moment, time's brief passing,
Look around and it's New Year.

Snow is falling, faster, faster:
Stepping out in rhythmic feet,
Tempo same and same the drag,
Might not with the selfsame beat
Time itself flit by and pass?
Might not all the years come and go
Like all the words knit into a poem,
Like the falling of the snow?

Snow is falling, snow is falling,
Snow is falling, all's a flurry—
Whitened walker in a hurry,
Flowers covered with surprise,
Corners where the crossroads rise.

IX

Forests and Mountains

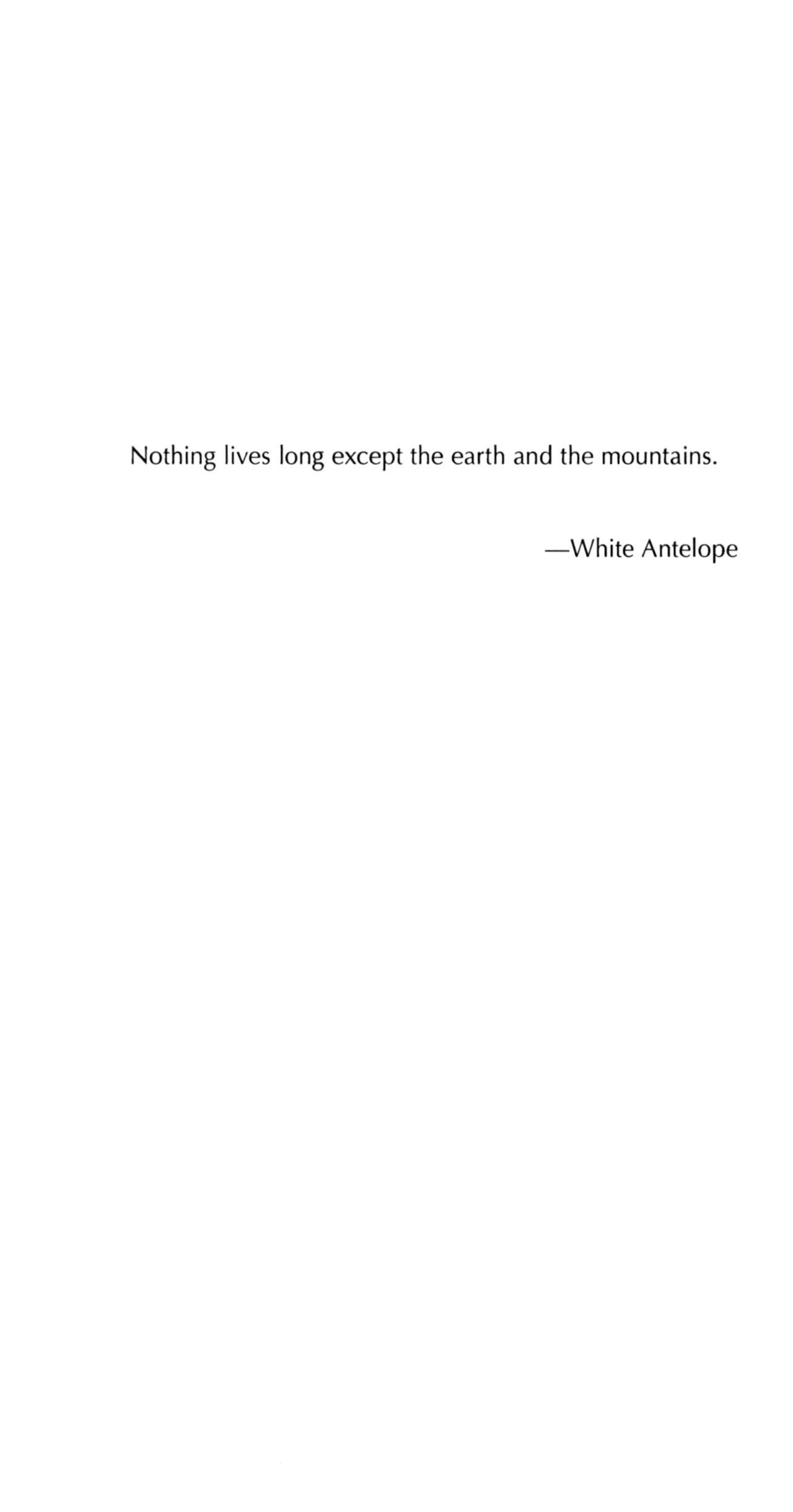

Nothing lives long except the earth and the mountains.

—White Antelope

September

Lauris Edmond

*This selection by New Zealand poet, Lauris Edmond (1924-2000), reflects her mind's deep penetration into the rural life that surrounded all her days. Edmond trained as a teacher, raised six children, and wrote poetry on the side. She published her first volume of poetry at age fifty (*In Middle Air*), to immediate acclaim, and over the next twenty-five years published thirteen more. September is spring in the Southern Hemisphere.*

The mountain leaps, and stands
breaking horizons. It is the first
land out of falling waters, the wind

finds it like a discovering dove.
in the wheeling light it is still,
construing containment, poise
from the inchoate idiom of the earth.

No flower was white before this
blossoming of snow, no September
sharp with spring until this morning.
I shall learn the lessons of God
from the mountain; it has entered
my imagination: eternal indifference,
eternal scope, eternal reprieve.

The Snowing of the Pines

Thomas Wentworth Higginson

In his retirement as a Civil War colonel in the first Black regimen from Massachusetts, Thomas Wentworth Higginson (1823-1911) spent his days at his home in Cambridge, observing nature and writing poetry.

SOFTER than silence, stiller than still air
Float down from high pine-boughs the slender leaves.
The forest floor its annual boon receives
That comes like snowfall, tireless, tranquil, fair.
Gently they glide, gently they clothe the bare
Old rocks with grace. Their fall a mantle weaves
Of paler yellow than autumnal sheaves
Or those strange blossoms the witch-hazels wear.
Athwart long aisles the sunbeams pierce their way;
High up, the crows are gathering for the night;
The delicate needles fill the air; the jay
Takes through their golden mist his radiant flight;
They fall and fall, till at November's close
The snow-flakes drop as lightly—snows on snows.

The Tree

John Haines

John Haines (b. 1924), Poet Laureate of Alaska, is also a naturalist and essayist who homesteaded for more than forty years along the Tanana River in Northern Alaska. His affinity with the natural world is evident in almost all his works. He said, "It is good to . . . sink one's fingers deep into the moss and feel the night and the frost that are waiting there; if for only a moment, to feel oneself once more at home on the earth."

Tree of my life,
you have grown slowly
in the shadow of giants.

Through darkness and solitude
you stretch year by year
towards that strange, clear light
in which the sky is hidden.

In the quiet grain of your
thoughts the inner life
of the forest stirs
like a secret still to be named.

The Tree of Goodness

Ch'ihwan Yu

Ch'ihwan Yu (1908-1967) was a high school teacher by profession but at heart a poet. He took his themes from nature which he learned to appreciate at first hand during World War II, when he wandered through Manchuria. In this sad poem Yu points to a critical dilemma of our age—a tree for firewood or for shade and sound? Usually the loggers win; fourteen million hectares of tropical forest are destroyed each year (an area nearly three times the size of Costa Rica).

By the roadside where I would roam stood an old pine
Spreading it dark limb carelessly aloft into space.
Even when windless, the tree would sigh so sadly
I used to stop awhile beneath it, happy
To hitch my thoughts with the sound of the pine
To the edge of the distant sky.
One day I found the tree cut down mercilessly.

Although the realities of life tempt us to take
The wood for heat rather than the shade and the sound
I stand in its place holding my arms high up into the air;
But I know not how to make my palm make
The profound sound of the tree.
Notwithstanding the divine music that sounds
From the remote sphere above my head
I grieve over the loss of the good tree.

The Parable of the Trees

The Dead Sea Scrolls

Translated by T. Carmi

This heavily symbolic parable comes from the Dead Sea Scrolls (c. 170 B.C.E.-c. 68 C.E.), which were discovered in 1947 by a Bedouin shepherd in a cave at Qumran, on the north-western shore of the Dead Sea. These manuscripts include the most ancient fragments of Hebrew Scriptures. "The Parable of the Trees" comes from the Hodayot *(i.e.* Thanksgiving Psalms*), hymns that resonate with biblical psalms. What do you make of this parable? How do you interpret it?*

I will praise you, O God, for you have put me by a source of streams on the dry ground, by the budding springs on the parched land, by the waters that irrigate your luxuriant garden—a grove of pine together with fir and box elder—which you planted for your glory. These are the Trees of Life, set beside a secret spring, concealed among all the well-watered trees.

One day the Trees of Life will put forth a shoot which will become the Everlasting Plant, for it will take root and extend roots towards the stream. And the plant will open its stem to the living waters. It will become an everlasting source of blessing. All the wild creatures will graze among its fallen leaves; all the wayfarers will pass by its stem; all the winged birds will nest in its boughs.

But now the Well-Watered Trees tower over it, for they grow as soon as they are planted; but their roots do not extend towards the stream. And the trees will one day put forth the holy shoot of the Plant of Truth—these trees are hidden away; their secret is sealed, it is not valued, it is not known. For you, O God, have hedged in its fruit on every side with the mystery of angels, creatures of might and of holy spirits, with a whirling, flashing fire.

No stranger can approach the spring of life; s/he cannot drink the holy waters together with the everlasting trees; s/he cannot bear fruit together with the heavenly plant—because s/he saw but did not understand; s/he considered but did not believe in the source of life; s/he dared to lay hands upon the eternal flower.

Hello Tree

Kath Walker

In this intriguing poem, contemporary Australian poet, Kath Walker, implores a tree to talk to her. Take a favorite tree that you know, or perhaps a glacial boulder, or even a grain of sand. Think for a few minutes and ask yourself what this tree or rock or tiny grain of sand would say to you if it had a voice.

Hello tree;
Talk to me.
I'm sick
And lonely.

Are you old?
Trunk so cold?
What secrets
Do you hold?

Talk tree!
Can't you see;
My troubles
Trouble me.

Silent tree
Let me see
Your answers.
ANSWER ME.

Tree!
You dare question ME?
How dare you
Dare, question ME?

Learn From the Pine

Bashō

Bashō (1644-1694), Japan's most famous poet, believed that contemplating and writing about ordinary elements and actions around him would lead to the deepening of all life experiences. He studied Japanese and Chinese classics and went to Edo (now Tokyo) to learn poetry and Zen. He became an extremely popular teacher whose students gave him his pen name from a luxuriant, broad-leafed banana tree his students gave him as a gift. "Learn from the Pines," one of Bashō's rare prose pieces, provides us with a well-phrased Zen way of meditating on nature.

Learn about pines from the pine, and about bamboo from the bamboo.

Make the universe your companion, always bearing in mind the true nature of things—mountains and rivers, trees and grasses, and humanity—and enjoy the falling blossoms and the scattering leaves.

It is this poetic spirit that leads one to follow nature and become a friend with things of the seasons. For a person who has the spirit, everything she sees becomes a flower, and everything he imagines turns into the moon.

Every form of insentient existence—plants, stones, or utensils—has its individual feelings similar to those of people. When we observe calmly, we discover that all things have their fulfillment.

Do Not Chop Me—I am Yours

Ghanshyam Sailani

Ghanshyam Sailani, is a folk singer, an environmental activist, and a devout Hindu. In "Do Not Chop Me—I Am Yours," he gives the tree voice, a voice pleading with the chain-saw crew and the clear cutters of the forest: "Do not chop me, I am yours. . . . I am milk and water to you. . . . I am the earth and life."

I have been standing for ages,
I wish to live for you.
Do not chop me, I am yours.
I wish to give you something in the future.
I am milk and water to you.
I am thick shade and showers.
I manufacture soil and manure.
Some of my kind bear fruits.
They ripen for you.
I wish to ripen with sweetness.
I wish to bow down to you.
I am the pleasant season.
I am spring. I am rains.
I am Earth and life.
I am everything to you.
Do not cut me, I have life,
I feel pain, so my name is tree.
Rolling of logs will create landslides.
Remember. I stand on slopes and below is the village.
Where we were destroyed,
Dust is flying there.
The hilltops have become barren.
All the water sources have dried up.
Do not cut us, save us.
Plant us, decorate the Earth.
What is ours is yours.
Leave something for posterity.

Any Fool Can Destroy Trees

John Muir

By the time "Any Fool Can Destroy Trees" came out, John Muir had been acknowledged as the country's the most ardent defender of the American wilderness. In 1876 he urged the federal government to adopt a forest conversation policy and he was largely responsible for the establishment of Sequoia and Yosemite National Parks in 1890. In doing so, Muir wrote, "I have done the best I could to show forth the beauty, grandeur, and all embracing usefulness of our wild mountain forest reservations and parks, with the view to inciting people to come and enjoy them, and get them into their hearts, so that at length their preservation and right use might be made sure."

The axe and saw are insanely busy, chips are flying thick as snowflakes, and every summer thousands of acres of priceless forests, with their underbrush, soil, springs, climate, scenery, and religion, are vanishing away in clouds of smoke.

Any fool can destroy trees. They cannot run away; and if they could, they would still be destroyed—chased and hunted down as long as fun or a dollar could be got out of their bark hides, branching horns, or magnificent bole backbones. Few that fell trees plant them; nor would planting avail much towards getting back anything like the noble primeval forests. During a lifetime only saplings can be grown, in the place of the old trees—tens of centuries old—that have been destroyed.

It took more than three thousand years to make some of the trees of these Western woods—trees that are still standing in perfect strength and beauty—waving and singing in the mighty forests of the Sierra. Through all the wonderful, eventful centuries since Christ's time—and long before that—God has cared for these trees, saved them from drought, disease, avalanches, and a thousand straining, leveling tempests and floods; but he cannot save them from fools.

Offering to Luna

Julia "Butterfly" Hill

On December 10, 1997, 23-year old Julia "Butterfly" Hill climbed to the top of a 1,000 year old, 200-foot tall redwood in northern California where she sat in the tree she called "Luna" for 738 day, vowing to protect it until the lumber company agreed to spare it. Julia's " sit" became the longest tree-sit in history. She said, "I gave my word to this tree, to the forest and all the people, that my feet would not touch the ground until I had done everything in my power to stop the destruction." The tree was saved.

A tree
a life so many years gone by
history bound in each new
ring and every scar
I lay nestles in Her arms
I listen to all She has to say
She speaks to me through my
Bare feet . . . my hands
She speaks to me on the
wind . . . and in the rain
telling me stories born long
before my time
Wisdom
As only Ancient Elders know
Truths
Passed to me through
Nature's perfect lips
She cries
Her overwhelming grief
Sap that clings to me . . .
To my soul
I wrap my arms around Her
Offering the only solace
That I know

Giving myself as the only gift
I have to give
A pitiful offering
To a Goddess such as this
But of myself
It is all that I have to give.

How Much Can I Learn From a Tree?

Satish Kumar

Satish Kumar was born on August 9, 1936, in Rajistan, India. The bombing of Nagasaki on his birthday in 1945 entered deeply into his consciousness. At 18, after reading about Gandhi's ideas on nonviolence, he dedicated himself to undertaking a peace walk from India to the four corners of the nuclear world: Moscow, Paris, London, and Washington. Calling it a "Pilgrimage for Peace," Kumar carried no money; he stayed with anyone who offered him food or shelter. The journey is chronicled in Kumar's book, No Destination.

Sometimes I came across a tree which seemed like a Buddha or a Jesus:
loving,
compassionate,
still,
unambitious,
enlightened,
in eternal meditation—
giving pleasure to a pilgrim,
shade to a cow,
berries to a bird,
beauty to its surroundings,
health to its neighbors,
branches for the fire,
leaves for the soil,
asking nothing in return,
in total harmony with the wind and the rain.
How much can I learn from a tree?

The tree is my church,
the tree is my temple,
the tree is my mantra,
the tree is my poem and my prayer.

The Waters of Life

Across the wall of the world,
A river sings a beautiful song—
Come rest here by my side.

—Maya Angelou,
"On the Pulse of Morning"

The Waterfall

Zhang Juiling

The T'ang Dynasty poet, Zhang Juiling (673-740), takes us to the edge of the waterfall. It is the springtime of the year and the stream is swollen with snow-melt. We hear the rushing wild torrent, carrying red soil and stones in its wake, crashing on the boulders below. We see the mist rise up and in a sudden shaft of light a rainbow is revealed. For just a moment, heaven and earth are meeting in a flash of cosmic beauty.

Out of the mists and the clouds with a leap
    and a shuddering cry
The waterfall, red with the blood of the earth,
    crashes to death with a sigh,
Down past the shivering trees to the rocks
    where its waters die
To arise in a vapor of ghostly forms
    seeking again the sky.
They weave from the threads of the sun
    a rainbow of tremulous light
While the sound of their dying sighs is
    the voice of a storm in its might.
The mountains in beauty dressed
    stand awed by that magical sight
Of the wedding of heaven and earth
    in a waterfall's headlong flight.

Happy Is the Eye That Sees Rain Pouring Down From Heaven

Moses Gabbai

Moses Gabbai (died c. 1443) was a rabbi in Majorca who ended his days in Algeria. This poem, based on the Mishnah (Jewish law which was codified in 200 C.E.), details ceremonies for invoking rain in a time of drought. It is ever contemporary since about a third of the earth's surface is either arid or semi-arid, impeding agriculture in some of the world's most impoverished nations.

Happy is the eye that sees all this!
We hear it and our soul rejoices.

Happy is the eye that sees water pouring down from heaven,
and the wind sweeping over the earth,
as the righteous one whispers to God, maker of lightening.
All the people stand before God murmuring sweet words.
We hear this and our soul rejoices.

Happy is the eye that sees the blackness of massed clouds
and the wind sweeping through with a downpour of blessings,
as the righteous one whispers to God who rides over the desert plains:
"Courage, my faithful ones, the clouds are pouring down water."
We hear this and our soul rejoices.

Happy is the eye that sees the glory of lightening
and thunders in hot pursuit,
with the winds sweeping over and all hearts struck with fear,
as the righteous one whispers to God, the Rock who dwells on high:
"Courage, my faithful ones, God is raining a downpour of blessings."
We hear this and our soul rejoices.

Happy is the eye that sees water in the streets and in the pathways,
and wind sweeping over to make the harvests bountiful

as the righteous one stands there, with water ever stronger,
pouring down the head, washing away the wood ashes,
drenching everything—
We hear this and our soul rejoices.

The Sound of Rain

Yohan Chu

Yohan Chu (1900-1979) was born in the north of Korea and educated both in Japan and China, where he studied the great masters of the T'ang and Sung dynasties whose influence is evident in "The Sound of Rain." His eloquent poetic imagery stimulates our imagination and the range of emotions we experience on a rainy day.

It is raining.
Night quietly unfolds her feathers;
Rain whispers in the yard like chickens
Peeping among themselves.

The moon going thread-thin,
Warm breezes start to rise as if
The spring trickles down from the stars.
Rain is falling this dark night.

Rain is raining
Gently like a kind guest calling.
I open the window to greet him;
Rain is raining, quiet and invisible.

It is raining in the yard,
Outside the window, on the roof.
Rain is raining to fetch glad tidings
For my private joy.

The River

Frederick George Scott

A Canadian Anglican priest, Frederick George Scott (1872-1934) was known as "The Poet of the Laurentians," mountains in Quebec where he lived and drew inspiration.

WHY hurry, little river,
Why hurry to the sea?
There is nothing there to do
But to sink into the blue
And all forgotten be.
There is nothing on that shore
But the tides for evermore,
And the faint and far-off line
Where the winds across the brine
For ever, ever roam
And never find a home.

Why hurry, little river,
From the mountains and the mead,
Where the graceful elms are sleeping
And the quiet cattle feed?
The loving shadows cool
The deep and restful pool;
And every tribute stream
Brings its own sweet woodland dream
Of the mighty woods that sleep
Where the sighs of earth are deep,
And the silent skies look down
On the savage mountain's frown.
Oh, linger, little river,
Your banks are all so fair,
Each morning is a hymn of praise,

Each evening is a prayer.
All day the sunbeams glitter
On your shallows and your bars,
And at night the dear God stills you
With the music of the stars.

Flowing Along the Border of Heaven

Li Po

The relationship between poetry and painting is well illustrated by Li Po's poem, "Flowing Along the Border of Heaven." Because of the intimate relationship between the two art forms, both of which speak to the innermost thoughts of the human soul, they are often combined on one scroll. Kuo Hsi, the celebrated artist of the Sung Dynasty whose paintings were said to be like the poems of Li Po (699-762), said that: "Poetry is a picture without form and painting is a poem with form.

My friend bids farewell at the Yellow Crane House,
And heads down eastwards to Willow Valley
Amid the flowers and mists of March.
The lonely sail in the distance
Vanishes at last beyond the blue sky
And I can see only the river
Flowing along the border of heaven.

Enchantments of the River

Paulo Gabriel

Paulo Gabriel, a popular singer in Brazil, has been described as a "builder of fantasies, dreamer of a new world, a mason of utopias."

You need to sail naked
through what is left of the forest
to discover what the earth was in the beginning.

And then penetrate, deeply moved,
through the spaces of light that the river offers
where the forest and the water balance,
wisely governed by the birds.

For it is only here where the earth
is not yet desecrated
that the ugly fear of death
spawned by human beings, does not reign.

On the beach, the turtle lays its eggs,
contemplated by the stork;
and on the sand the alligator rests,
serious, like a general in uniform.
The tortoise spies from the woods;
wild ducks and toucans drink the morning breeze
while a band of yellow butterflies announce
that the world is fragile, like a dance.

Along the riverbank, searching for water,
roots reveal the direction of life.
It seems that goodness passed through the world
before consciousness was perverted.

Today I don't want to meet anyone,
just stay by the river forever,
to judge without hurting it,
the true dimension of the earth.

River Wind

Brian Turner

The New Zealand contemporary poet, Brian Turner (b. 1944), won the Commonwealth Poetry Prize for his first volume of poems, Ladders of Rain, *and the New Zealand Book Award for Poetry in 1993. Recently he has been able to say "writing is what I do," but for a long time his writing was fitted around his work as customs officer, publishers rep, journalist, editor, worker in saw mills and on construction sites. He is an out-of-doors person—a fly fisherman, a cricketer, a mountaineer. He is most comfortable in the cathedral of the forest where, in this poem, he imagines the wind talking to the river.*

The wind may let us down
but it never fails. The wind
carries dark clouds
on its shoulders
and totters down
from the mountains.

And there comes a time
when all hills
are mountains. Now is the time.
If rain is to fall
let it fall gently
on the shoulders of the mountains,
and let it run quietly
and quickly
into the river
that feels the light in the sky
and prizes the light.

Instinctively
you know what the river is saying
without being told. You hear
what the river is singing
without knowing the words
to the song. You know where
the river is going
and that it doesn't know
what you know, that it tempts you
to envy
and the feeling returns and returns.

Water, My Sister Water

Helder Camara

This and the other poems from Dom Helder Camara's little book, Sister Earth, are very reminiscent of St. Francis of Assisi's "Canticle of Brother Sun," written in the early thirteenth century. Camara was a modern day St. Francis, a champion of the poorest and a man in love with the earth.

When you were created
Did you yet know
How many would be
The things you must do,
From the most noble
And beautiful
To the most base
And desolate?

Yes, you are beautiful
In the stillness of lakes,
(As humble brooks
Or as the rushing rapids),
In glittering cascades,
In the oceans which leave in us
The lingering images of
The infinite.

Yet for those who have eyes to see
And ears to hear,
You are still more beautiful
As you labor, with joy,
On your round of lowly tasks:
The washing of clothes,
The cleaning of floors,
The quenching of imperious thirst.

And impressive are you
In your ceaseless travel,
Lifted from the earth to the clouds,
And coming down again from heaven,
To bring life
To the plants,
To the animals,
Life to the human race.

How did you receive
The dreadful commission
To bring the flood
And storms at sea
And wild lashing of the tempest?
Do you know
You give the chance
Of heaven as the reward
Of those who offer you
To quench the thirst
Of their brother of sister?

Do you know
The sins of the human race
Are to blame
For the many pains
You are forced to cure?

Thank you,
Sister Water.

Forgive
Us who make you
Perform cruel tasks.

Thank you,
Above all
Because you help us
To praise
The Creator and Father.

Sitting by the Sea

Jane Resture

The Republic of the Marshall Islands is a turquoise sea world of 1,225 islands grouped in twenty-nine low-lying, fragile coral atolls, now threatened by rising sea levels. The poem's author, Jane Resture, has said: "So much of the old world created by our island ancestors has passed away. Members of the divine family of the Sky-father and the Earth-mother are still with us even though so many of the symbols of our spiritualism have been scattered among museums around the world. What the future holds may be unclear particularly when the ocean may claim many of our islands. Perhaps by reclaiming our cultural values we can understand who we are and what the future may hold for our people of Oceania."

I sit by the sea
And let the waves talk to me
With stories of days gone by
About seafarers of old and sailors so bold
And frigate birds high in the sky.
The lapping of the waves
Recalls better days
When our people were free to roam
The great oceans wide
With the wind and stars as our guide
Looking for some place called home.
Those mythical men
We will never see again
And gods that we still call our own
How the world came to be

For people like me
Where our spirits forever did roam.
Now the waves on the shore
Don't seem the same any more
Their stories full of grief
Are filled with a warning
About global warming and its consequences
For our people on the reef.
Yet I still sit by the sea
While the waves talk to me
With stories of days gone by
About seafarers of old and sailors right bold
And frigate birds high in the sky.

XI

Creatures Great and Small

The wolf shall live with the lamb, and the leopard shall lie down with the kid, the calf and the young lion shall grow up together, and a little child shall lead them.

—Isaiah 11:6

Ask the Animals

Job 12

Paraphrase by Anne Rowthorn

We are privileged to share our planet with birds and fish and every kind of animal that inhabits the land. Do we regard them, as Job and St. Francis did, as our brothers and sisters in creation? Do they have knowledge and intelligence that human beings do not possess? Do animals have rights? Do they have feelings? What is our responsibility in protecting them and insuring their welfare?

Ask the animals,
 and they will teach you.

Ask the birds of the air,
 and they will tell you.

Ask the planets of the earth,
 and they will inform you.

Ask the fish of the sea,
 and they will declare to you.

Who among you does not know
 that the hand of God has done all this?

In God's hand is the life of every living thing,
 and the breath of every human being.

The Eagle

Alfred, Lord Tennyson

With "The Eagle," composed in 1851, Tennyson (1809-1892) invites us to close our eyes and imagine a vast windswept land, to hear the howling of the wind against the barren branches, and there to picture the majestic eagle perched against the azure sky, out of which he falls "like a thunderbolt."

He clasps the crag with crooked hands;
Close to the sun in lonely lands,
Ringed with the azure world, he stands.

The wrinkled sea beneath him crawls;
He watches from his mountain walls,
And like a thunderbolt he falls.

Bees

Luo Yin

Luo Yin (833-909), a poet of T'ang Dynasty, wrote simple and popular yet provocative poetry. In "Bees" Luo Yin asks the question as to who the works of creation are for. What purpose do they serve? Is the toil of the bee for its own glory? What place does the bee have in the wider scheme of nature? The humble bee is an insect of great power. Its sting has been known to kill a giant; its honey delights the palates of princes.

Down in the plain, and up on the mountain top,
All nature's boundless glory is their prey.
But when they have sipped from a hundred flowers
 and made honey,
For whom is this toil, for whom this nectar?

The Great Blue Heron

Author Unknown

The great blue heron is the city bird of Portland, Oregon. This poem appears on a plaque at Portland City Hall.

Out of their loneliness for each other
two reeds, or maybe two shadows, lurch
forward and become suddenly a life
lifted from dawn or the rain. It is
the wilderness come back again, a lagoon
with our city reflected in its eye.
We live by faith in such presences.
It is a test for us, that thin
but real, undulating figure that promises,
"If you keep faith I will exist
at the edge, where your vision joins
the sunlight and the rain: heads in the light,
feet that go down in the mud where truth is."

Elephant

Yoruba Oral Tradition

Author Unknown

There are many different versions of this Yoruba chant from Nigeria, but they all express admiration and wonder at this huge animal's qualities. It is said that the spirit of Africa always appears as an elephant because no other animal can vanquish it, not even a lion.

Elephant, opulent creature,
Elephant, huge as a hill, even when kneeling,
Elephant, robed in honor who splinters the tree branches.
Mountainous animal, huge beast, who tears a man like a garment
 and hangs him on a tree.
At the sight of him people stampede to safety.
My chant is a salute to the elephant:

Elephant, massive blackish-gray creature,
Elephant, who single-handed makes the dense forest tremble.
Elephant, who stands sturdy and upright, who strolls as if reluctantly,
Hunter's boast home is not repeated when he meets the elephant.
Elephant, who has a head pad but carries no load,
Elephant, whose burden is the huge head he balances,
Learn from the elephant.

Honor's equal,
Elephant who constantly swings his trunk like a fly-whisk,
Elephant, whose eyes are like water-jars,
Elephant, the greatest of wanderers, whose teeth are a big as palm oil
 pits,
Elephant, lord of the forest,
Elephant, whose tusks are like shafts,
One of whose tusks is a porter's whole load,
Elephant with the mighty neck,

Elephant, whom the hunter sometimes sees face to face,
Elephant, whom the hunter at other times sees from the rear,
Elephant, you carry mortars, yet walk with a swaggering fait,
    treading ponderously.

Thank You, Zebra

Shona Oral Tradition

Author Unknown

"Thank You Zebra" is an extract from a Shona praise poem from Chihota's clan in Zimbabwe. For Chihota's people, the zebra is a metaphor for the qualities of the clan.

Thank you, Zebra,
Adorned with your own stripes,
Iridescent and glittering creature,
Whose skin is as soft as girls' is;
One on which the eye dwells all day;
Creature that makes the forests beautiful,
Weaver of lines
Who wear your skin for display,
Drawn with the lines so clearly defined;
You who thread beads in patterns,
Beauty spot cut to rise is a crescent on the forehead,
A patterned belt for the waist;
Light reflected,
Dazzling the eyes.
It is its own instinct, the Zebra's,
Adorned as if with strings of beads around the waist as women are;
Wild creature without anger or any grudge,
Lineage with a totem that is nowhere a stranger,
Line that stretches everywhere,
Owners of the land.

Buffalo, We Salute You

Yoruba Oral Tradition

Author Unknown

This Yoruba poem from Nigeria vividly describes the buffalo's attributes of speed and lightness (the butterfly image) and terrifying strength (roaring like a rainstorm). The hunter knew the buffalo well and had tremendous respect for it.

Buffalo, we salute you:
Butterfly of the savannah
    skimming along without touching the grass:
Corpulent beat, equally at home in the thick forest
    and in the wooded plain:
The hunter prostrates himself before you.
Hunters pose ceremoniously on the head
    of the elephant they have just killed,
But who would dare pose on the head of a fallen buffalo,
    the raging buffalo of the bone-hard horns?
Let the hunter give up pursuing the buffalo,
    in case the beast accidentally devours him like grass.
Buffalo, who frightens the young hunter,
    making him scramble up even the thorniest tree,
    who has razors at the tip of his horns:
Buffalo, ancient beast, when you hear roaring and there is no rain,
    there is the buffalo!

The Peaceful Earth

Isaiah 11

Paraphrase by Anne Rowthorn

The prophet Isaiah anticipates a time when all humanity and every creature of the natural world will be reconciled, when ancient enemies will be sharing a love feast, when the earth will be "full of the knowledge of our Holy God."

The wolf shall live with the lamb,
and the leopard with the kid.
The calf and the lion shall feed together.
The cow and the bear will be friends.
Their young shall lie down together.
The lion will eat straw like the ox.
The infant will play safely over the cobra's hole.
The young child shall put its hand on the adder's den.
They will neither hurt nor destroy on all my holy mountain.
For the whole earth will be full of the knowledge
    of our Holy God
    just as the waters cover the sea.

The Animals Speak to Us

Indian Center of Blue Cloud Abbey

Author Unknown

Historically the Lakota gave animals utmost respect, regarding them as kindred beings of Earth. They still do. Animals' lives are precious and have value in themselves, apart from their value to humans. As we walked to his sweat lodge, a Lakota man in Pine Ridge, South Dakota, warned me to watch my step. "The ants are my little pets," he said, and he meant it. While the Lakota would kill the buffalo for food and clothing, they did so soberly in the realization that in doing so, they were robbing the animal of its life.

"The animals speak to us," the Lakota say. Sometimes, if a person is willing to listen and look quietly, animals will come around and bring a message. It might be a little bird in the top of a tree, a rabbit hopping by, or even an ant. Even a prairie dog who pops his head out of his hole may have something to tell us. If these animals are not respected, like the buffalo, they may disappear from the Earth. Then the Lakota and all people will be without their message forever.

Animals were created by the Great Spirit first, before people were put on the Earth. Thus they are closer to God. They helped to get Earth ready for people to live on. They were told to sacrifice themselves for others, so that people might have something to eat. The Lakota always offer an apology for killing their "relatives" the animals, and pray in thanksgiving for the food they give.

Animals are also very simple and pure. They have their own code put in them by the Great Spirit, and they always live according to that code. In the fall the geese know it is time to get together and fly south. Other animals know when it is time to dig back into Mother Earth and let her keep them warm during the winter. Animals are kind to their little ones and protect them by putting themselves in danger. They only take and use what they need to survive.

The Song of the Universe

When we hear the warbling of the mountain thrush in the blossoms or the voice of the frog in the water, we know that every living being has a song.

—Ki no Tsurayuki,
Kokinshū

Mountain Chant

Navajo Chant

Author Unknown

The "Mountain Chant" with its many variations, is a chant of the beautyway (life span), which is sung for several purposes. It is part of the puberty rite performed with Navajo children when they come of age. It is sung while traveling anywhere but especially over the mountains, as a prayer that the traveler will be at one with the birds and animals with the rocks and grasses, with the sky and clouds along the way. It is chanted when a person is out of balance with life and needs to be brought back in harmony with the universe.

The voice that beautifies the land!
The voice above,
The voice of the thunder,
Among the dark clouds
Again and again it sounds,
The voice that beautifies the land!

The voice that beautifies the land!
The voice below,
The voice of the grasshopper,
Among the flowers and grasses
Again and again it sounds,
The voice that beautifies the land!

Lines Written in Early Spring

William Wordsworth

William Wordsworth (1770-1850) was one of the great poets of England's Romantic Age in which nature was rediscovered and glorified. Reading this poem, one can almost see Wordsworth resting in a stand of woods in his beloved Lake District, trying to imagine what it is like to be a flower enjoying the air it breathes, or a bird at play. He opens his ears to the music of the universe where he hears ". . . a thousand blended notes. . . ."

I heard a thousand blended notes,
While in a grove I sat reclined,
In that sweet mood when pleasant thoughts
Bring sad thoughts to mind.

To her fair works did Nature link
The human soul that through me ran;
And much it grieved my heart to think
What man has made of man.

Through primrose tufts, in that green bower,
The periwinkle trailed its wreaths;
And 'tis my faith that every flower
Enjoys the air it breathes.

The birds around me hopped and played,
Their thoughts cannot measure—
But the least motion which they made,
It seemed a thrill of pleasure.
The budding twigs spread out their fan,
To catch the breezy air;
And I must think, do all I can,
That there was pleasure there.

If this belief from heaven be sent
If such be Nature's holy plan,
Have I not reason to lament
What man has made of man?

Sound

Kijo Song

Traditional Korean poetry is influenced by the writings of the Chinese landscape poets as is evident in this contemporary poem by Kijo Song, born in 1932. Song encourages readers to listen to the natural world.

I must go to the mountains
to hear
the sound of a brook
that's been breathing, ambushed,
under snow all winter
the sound of snow melting and ice defreezing
the sound of the spring opening
a breath crawling on the earth

The sound of trees growing
the sound of grass growing
the sound of flowers opening bud
the sound of sunlight getting wedged in the rocks

I must go to the mountains
to hear
the sound and the sound.

Sounds Assail Me

Kath Walker

Kath Walker—Australian poet, educator, environmentalist, and human rights activist—articulated the feelings of a whole generation of Australian Aboriginal people. She was instrumental in getting the vote for her people (1967). Even though she became a city-dweller, she never lost her ear for the "sounds God made," the natural rhythms of nature.

Something obscene
In man-made sounds affronts the sweet and clean,
But nature's never.
Shout of the stormy winds, ever
Toneless and rude, tossing the trees,
The harsh scream of seabirds—these
Somehow belong
As much as the wren's airy song.
Man only, the books tell, knows evil and wrong;
Even as art now the yelp and the yell
Like music of hell,
Music made evil, the squawk and squall
When the disc jockeys loose the blare and bawl.
Give me the sounds God made so—
I love them all
Whether loud or low,
From the small, thin
Note of the bee's violin
To the rough sea's uproar,
In wild tumult tumbling upon the shore.

Silence

Peter Gold

The ancients of Asia often believed that the gods descended to earth from mountain tops. Even modern poets find power and a sense of holiness in high and quiet places "atop the altar of the earth."

The occasional bleat of a sheep,
    bang of a bell,
    a snatch of song by a villager harvesting her field,
    are all that one can hear.

Otherwise, silence.

Silence, like an infinity view down the spreading valley.
Silence, like the clouds gathering momentarily above it.
Silence, like the sandy gullies that turn into boiling torrents
    when the heavy rains eventually come.
Silence, like the narrow lane curling around one mountain's base
    then the next.
Silence, like the wildflowers subtly swaying
    to the touch of an unseen breeze.
Silence, golden like the sun now beginning to flood the landscape
    with warmth, bringing life wherever it goes.
Silence, in solitude, brings one great solace,
    atop the altar of the earth.

Beauty in a Moment

almost at the equator
almost at the equinox
exactly at midnight
from a ship
the full
moon
in the center of the sky.

—Gary Snyder,
"Only Once"

Between the Embers and the Stars

Erazim Kohák

Th Czech philosopher, Erazim Kohák, tells us that he has sought "... to articulate faithfully the moral sense of nature and of being human therein through the seasons lived in the solitude of the forest, beyond the power line and the paved road, where the dusk comes softly and there still is night, pure between the glowing embers and the distant stars."

Once more it is autumn, when the sun grows golden with the turning leaves and the air heavy with fruition and decay. Somewhere the grapes grow rich on the vine. The leaves of the red maple, whose color all summer anticipates the fall, grow tan; the fresh pine straw softly blankets the corner of memories beneath the white pines. Around the clearing the forest floor lights up with the gold of freshly fallen leaves; the river bed is bright with them beneath the clear water. . . .

. . . The fulfillment of life cannot be in its future. That future is always an end. We know that. We ought not to wonder that something perishes. We hurt when we forget that the point of life is not that it should last forever. Its overlooked wonder is that it once was; there once was a human being; there once was a raccoon. That is the miracle, that is the point.

The golden leaves line the river bottom, setting the water aglow in the autumn sun. The forest dies and is renewed in the order of time; the sparkling river bears away grief. In the pained cherishing of that transient world, the human, a dweller between the embers and the stars, can rise up to eternity. That is the task of humans. The moral sense of nature is that it can teach us to cherish time and to look to eternity within it.

Flower in the Crannied Wall

Alfred, Lord Tennyson

Alfred, Lord Tennyson (1809-1892) has been called the "Spokesman of the Victorian Age." One of twelve children of a parson, Tennyson only ever wanted to be a poet and, in fact, his first volume of poems was published when he was just eighteen. His whole being was conditioned by rural rather than urban life. He possessed the country person's awe at the splendor of something so small as a flower growing out of a crack in a wall.

Flower in the crannied wall,
I pluck you out of the crannies,
I hold you here, root and all, in my hand,
Little flower—but if I could understand
What you are, root and all, and all in all,
I should know what God and man is.

The Far Echoes of the Tides

Du Xunhe

Du Xunhe (late 9th c.) was a poet of the late T'ang era. "The Far Reaches of the Tides" illustrates the classical Chinese poet's way of trapping a moment's vision within just a few lines. There is a lot of room between the artfully applied words for the reader to fill in the spaces and become part of this evening landscape. It is as if we were sitting quietly beside the poet watching "the flower-like moon and the sparkling stars fade from the sky."

I sit and watch
The flower-like moon
And the sparkling stars
Fade from the sky.
The shadows of the mountains
And the far echoes of the tides.

Every Petal, Every Speck

Liu Kezhuang

Liu Kezhuang (1187-1269) was a highly respected poet of the Sung Dynasty. This poem expresses a comprehensive sense of God's presence in every aspect of creation, from the tiniest petal to the wind's mightiest blast.

Every petal is light as the butterfly's raiment;
Every speck is blood-red and tiny.
If you say that god cares not for the flowers,
Consider the hundred kinds and the thousand varieties,
    skillfully fashioned.
At morn you see the tree tops luxuriant,
At eve you see the branch-tops denuded.
If you say that God, in truth, cares for the flowers,
Consider the rain's drenching, and the wind's blast.

In the Sixth Month

Selected haiku from the works of Bashō

Translated by R. H. Blyth

By the age of thirty-four, Bashō had become the leader of a group of young poets at the center of the literary life of the capital (Edo, later Tokyo). Although he was cherished by his students, he was by nature a shy loner. He wearied of the lifestyle of a professional poet and in his forties he embarked on a wandering life, staying at monasteries and country houses, writing as he went.

In the sixth month
Mount Arashi
lays clouds on its summit.

Harvest moon—
walking around the pond
all night long.

A petal shower
of mountain roses,
and the sound of rapids.

Coolness of the melons
flecked with mud
in the morning dew.

Winter solitude—
in a world of one color
the sound of wind.

The hollyhocks
lean toward the sun
in May rain.

The dragonfly
can't quite land
on that blade of grass.

A field of cotton—
as if the moon
had flowered.

Soil

Richard H. Goodwin

Richard Goodwin (1910-2007), author of this poem, addresses the soil. The poem is on a plaque adorning a glacial boulder in the Burnham Brook Preserve, a forested hiking area with rocky ledges traversed by the Eight Mile River. Dick Goodwin, a botany professor at Connecticut College, was co-founder of the Nature Conservancy in Connecticut. The property that was to become the Burnham Brook Preserve was one of the first parcels given to the Nature Conservancy in Connecticut.

Soil
Dark, moist, wonder in my hand,
Living, breathing, nurse of seed,
Foundation of all,
How many dead leaves have you known?
How many men?
The peace you must have known,
Having flown as a bird,
Leaped as a frog,
Thought as a man,
Loved as a woman.
Eternal life or living dead,
When I am to be set among you,
Cast my ash with the wildest of daisies.

Looking Deeply

Thich Nhat Hanh

Thich Nhat Hanh, the author of "Looking Deeply," is a greatly revered Vietnam-born Zen master who is also a poet and peace activist. He believes that, in order to live our lives connected with the forces of the universe, we need to be able to look deeply into the heart of creation—to BE the river, to BE the forest, to BE the sun and stars. Doing so, we will become our true selves and look to the future with hope and expectation.

We need to look deeply at things in order to see. When a swimmer enjoys the clear water of a river, he or she should also be able to be the river. If we want to continue to enjoy our rivers—to swim in them, walk beside them, even drink their water—we have to meditate on being the river. If we cannot feel the rivers, the mountains, the air, the animals, and other people from within their own perspective, the rivers will die and we will lose our chance for peace.

If you are a mountain climber or someone who enjoys the countryside, or the green forest, you know that the forests are our lungs outside our bodies, just as the sun is our heart outside our bodies. Yet we have been acting in a way that has allowed two million square miles of forest land to be destroyed by acid rain, and we have destroyed parts of the ozone layer that regulate how much direct sunlight we receive. We are imprisoned in our small selves, thinking only of the comfortable conditions of this smaller self, while we destroy our larger self. We need to be able to be our true self. This means being able to be the river, to be the forest, the sun and the ozone layer. Thus we will be able to understand and have hope for the future.

What A Wonderful World

William Blake

When William Blake was a child he had a vision in which he saw God looking at him through the window. The vision carried his eye beyond the window to a tree outside, a tree that was full of angels. This vision never left him, and Blake was to have many more visions throughout his life. He trusted them as bearers of truth; they were the source of his inspiration. Blake claimed that he first painted his visions and later wrote down words to accompany the paintings that had been dictated to him by God. "I copy imagination," he said. "I write when commanded by the spirits." There is a distinctly—although almost certainly unintended—Zen quality to this poem, a looking deeply into something so ordinary as a grain of sand and in it seeing the universe.

To see a World in Grain of Sand
and a Heaven in a Wild Flower,
hold Infinity in the palm of your hand
and Eternity in an hour.

XIV

Remembrance, Regret, and Requiem

My heart is moved by all I cannot save; so much has been destroyed. I have cast my lot with those who age after age, perversely, with no extraordinary power, reconstitute the world.

—Adrienne Rich,

The Dream of a Common Language

It Should Be Visible

Denise Levertov

Following his first flight around the Earth, the German astronaut, Sigmund Jahn, wrote, " . . . only when I saw our vulnerable planet from space, in all its ineffable beauty and fragility, did I realize that humankind's most urgent task is to cherish and preserve it for future generations." Denise Levertov's haunting poem, "It Should Be Visible" resonates with this point of view.

If from Space not only sapphire continents,
swirling oceans, were visible, but the wars—
like bonfires, wildfires, forest conflagrations,
flame and smoky smoulder—the Earth would seem
a bitter pomander ball bristling with poison cloves.
And each war fuelled with weapons: it should be visible
that great sums of money have been exchanged,
great profits made, workers gainfully employed
to construct destruction, national economies distorted
so that these fires, these wars, may burn
and consume the joy of this planet
which, seen from outside its transparent tender shell,
is so serene, so fortunate, with its water, air
and myriad forms of 'life that wants to live.'
It should be visible that this bluegreen globe
suffers a canker which is devouring it.

The Book of Endings

Sam Taylor

The contemporary American poet, Sam Taylor, lives in the mountains of Northern New Mexico. He teaches at the University of New Mexico-Taos and is the caretaker of a wildlife refuge. The rate of species going extinct was ten to twenty-five a year but in recent years 784 species of plants and animals have gone extinct, among them the golden coqui, a Puerto Rican tree frog, the Martinique parrot, and the Madagascar Pygmy hippo.

Some time while you read this page
or the next one, a species—
a species as vast as your life
and the lives of all your ancestors
chasing bison across Old Europe
or huddled around a fire—will disappear.
A species that has found its own
ways of eating, of moving, of hiding
from predators; a species
that meets itself and makes love
in the bark of a tree or on the leaves
of the canopy or in the humid dirt.
And it has come with us for millions
of years, for millions of years,
it has watched the night
and day follow each other, it has breathed
with the frogs, it has wrapped
the stars around it like a blanket,
a patterned music, a map.
At the beginning of this page
there may have been three or four left,
but now there is only one.
And if you read this page again,
it will be another one, another species,
another story of four billion years

telling itself for the last time.
Wherever life began—a word, a wish
breathed into water, a seed falling
through space—it was all of us
there—as it is now
in this unknown last one.
It has bored into wood, it has carried
water on its back, it has drunk
the dew from its back in the desert,
it has fed its young with strips of
leaves, it has built homes out of bark,
it has caged the sky into a song,
it has spoken in ways no man has heard.
it has emerald wings
it has sapphire wings
it has wings of night
you will never see it
it is already gone.

Time Is Running Out

Kath Walker

Not only was Australian poet Kath Walker an ardent defender of Aboriginal rights, she was an environmentalist who believed that the land also has rights. Time is running out. In this poem she urges people to take a stand for the love of land.

The miner rapes
The heart of earth
With his violent spade.
Stealing, bottling her black blood
For the sake of greedy trade.
On his metal throne of destruction,
He labors away with a will,
Piling the mountainous minerals high
With giant tools and iron drill.

In his greedy lust for power,
He destroys nature's will.
For the sake of the filthy dollar,
He dirties the nest he builds.
Well he knows that violence
Of his destructive kind
Will be violently written
Upon the sands of time.

But time is running out
And time is close at hand,
For the Dreamtime folk are massing
To defend their timeless land.
Come gentle black man
Shown your strength;
Time to take a stand/
Make the violent miner feel
Your violent
Love of land.

Seven Days

J. R. Roland

The contemporary Australian poet, J. R. Roland, presents a chilling reversal of the familiar Genesis story of God creating the world in seven days. It is a solemn warning that all of creation as we know it today could become "a thousand eons without a word." It does not have to happen. We can stop the clock and start living as ecologically responsible citizens of creation. The choice is ours.

Thunder moved in sleep,
Birds dropped from the sky, white-eyed,
Every animal died
The evening of the first day.
Fish curdled the sea
Whales panting on their side
Clogging the uneven tide
The evening of the second day.
On the third day the stars
Darkened, sun and moon
Ending their alternate reign.
The fourth day the last leaf
Perished, herb and seed
Shriveled from the flayed
Earth. Water and land
Merged on the fifth day, on the sixth
Darkness and light. The seventh
Became a thousand eons without a word.

The End of Nature

Bill McKibben

Human "progress" and ingenuity have changed the atmosphere, and the atmosphere is changing the weather. Temperature and rainfall are no longer the work of some separate, untamable force, but instead a product of our habits, our economies, our way of life.

An idea, a relationship, can go extinct, just as an animal or a plant. The idea in this case is "nature," the separate and wild province, the world apart from humankind, to which s/he adapted, under whose rules s/he was born and died. In the past, we spoiled and polluted parts of that nature, inflicting environmental damage. But that was like stabbing a person with toothpicks: though it hurt, annoyed, degraded, it did not touch vital organs, block the path of the lymph or blood. We never thought that we had wrecked nature. Deep down, we never really thought we could: it was too big and too old; it's forces—the wind, the rain, the sun—were too strong, too elemental.

But, quite by accident, it turned out that the carbon dioxide and other gases we were producing in our pursuit of a better life—in pursuit of warm houses and eternal economic growth and of agriculture so productive it would free most of us from farming—could alter the power of the sun, could increase its heat. And that could increase its heat. And that increase could change the patterns of moisture and dryness, breed storms in new places, breed deserts. Those things may or may not have yet begun to happen, but it too late to altogether prevent them from happening. We have produced the carbon dioxide—we are ending nature.

We have not ended rainfall or sunlight; in fact rainfall and sunlight may become more important forces in our lives. It is too early to tell exactly how much harder the wind will blow, how much hotter the sun will shine. That is for the future. But the meaning of the wind, the sun, the rain—of nature—has already changed. Yes, the wind still blows—but no longer from some other sphere, some inhuman place.

We Have Forgotten Who We Are

United Nations Environmental Sabbath Program

Based on Words of Chief Seattle

This prayer, based on the words of Chief Seattle, asks us to confront what humankind has done to disfigure the planet and to recover from deep down in our primordial past a time when our forebears did love and respect our precious Mother Earth. Having recovered our memory we can work to heal God's creation so it may recover its splendor.

We have forgotten who we are.
We have alienated ourselves from the unfolding of the cosmos.
We have become estranged from the movements of the earth.
We have turned our backs on the cycles of life.

We have forgotten who we are
We have sought only our own security.
We have exploited simply for our own ends.
We have distorted our knowledge.
We have abused our power.

We have forgotten who we are.
Now the land is barren
And the waters are poisoned
And the air is polluted.

We have forgotten who we are.

Now the forests are dying
And the creatures are disappearing,
And the humans are despairing.

We have forgotten who we are.
We ask forgiveness.
We ask for the gift of remembering.
We ask for the strength to change.

We have forgotten who we are.

When the Last Leaf Falls

Tove

A Netherlands-based organization, Peace Child International, sent questionnaires to children in sixty countries asking them what an ideal book on the environment would contain. The result was the 1992 publication of the Children's State of the World Handbook, *a colorful book full of children's drawings, poems, essays, and suggestions for improving the quality of Planet Earth. Tove, a young person from Sweden, contributed this poem.*

When the last leaf falls,
When the last drop of water dries out,
When the ozone layer is already destroyed,
Will it be too late to understand
that money is not going to save us?

Take One Last Look

Aditi Charda

Dissatisfied with the results of the United Nations Conference on Environment and Development in 1992, members of UNICEF asked young people from every corner of the world what they felt the conference should have achieved and what they thought about the future of Mother Earth. Aditi Charda, a young person from Tanzania, contributed this poem to a UNICEF-sponsored book, which presents the views and opinions of youth and their concerns for the planet.

Take a seat under a tree
and let the stillness envelop you.
let the liana softly stroke your hair
as you watch patches of sunlight
dancing on the fallen leaves.

Listen carefully and you will hear
the gurgling of a nearby stream,
the chat of monkeys
in the branches above you.

Look carefully and you will see
the verdant green of young shoots
straining towards
the sunlight.
You will notice the bright
splashes of tiny red and
yellow flowers.
Look long and hard,
for you will want to be able to remember
and describe this to your grandchildren
when you return many years from now
and find a bare,
arid desert.

Death

Aleksandra Warzecka

Anyone experiencing a decaying chemical industrial site would understand exactly what Aleksandra Warzecka, a seventeen-year-old Polish boy, is talking about. "To break this invisible chain of death," according to Lester Brown, founder of the World Watch Institute, "depends on more of us becoming environmental activists, working on behalf of the future of the planet and our children."

Crushed by burden of lead
    I breathe in the black particles of
    invisible death.
    They are surrounding me,
    surrounding me from all sides.
I keep them away
    with the movement of my hand.
I don't see them but
    they are still in a terrible nearness,
    hidden in mysterious words:
    dioxins,
    phenol,
    nitrogen oxides.
Death is lurking,
    encircling every particle of air.
It kills and kills cruelly
    with a black chain which surrounds
    my head,
    my hands,
    my mind.
Death comes with acid rain,
    turning our world into something monstrous:
    mutated trees,
    dead animals,
    black dust swirling over my head.

I am looking for the greenness
    and for the normal trees,
    people unchanged into crazies.
But only the black smoke do I have in sight,
    clouds heavy with poison.
    there is invisible death lurking in them,
    invisible death,
    invisible death.
    DEATH.

A Day Comes When Dust Shall Darken the Air

Mayan Tradition

Author Unknown

This prophesy comes from one of the books of Chilan Balan, *the Mayan chronicles recorded in the fifteenth century before the arrival of the gold-seeking Europeans. Sadly, the prophecy has come to pass.*

Eat, eat, while there is bread,
Drink, drink, while there is water;
A day comes when dust shall darken the air,
When a blight shall wither the land,
When a cloud shall arise,
When a mountain shall be lifted us,
When a strong man shall seize the city,
When ruin shall fall upon all things,
When the tender leaf shall be destroyed,
When eyes shall be closed in death;
When there shall be three signs on a tree,
Father, son and grandson hanging dead on the same tree;
When the battle flag shall be raised,
And the people scattered abroad in the forests.

Requiem For What We Once Had

Edith Shiffert

Along with the writer of this dark poem, we get glimpses of apocalyptic times—droughts, uncontrollable fires, searing summer heat, floods, rising seas. As lovers of the earth we can all remember a more pristine world. But we also know that memory leads to hope and hope to action. It is up to us. We can choose life or death, blessing or curse. Either we take action or destine ourselves to "solitary tears."

If this beloved world is dying
say your farewells with tears of despair,
and say them clearly.
The mountains we have trashed, the seas, the fields,
remember them at their best
but know they disintegrate back to dark spaces and fires,
falling, falling, into the eternities of silence again
from which they began.

And hold your cherishing carefully.
Perhaps it can be used again.
Shreds saved from grief and knowledge
might resurrect as dusts, fragments, seeds,
and one locust emerge years from now
out of storm-torn clouds, black vapors, draught, and lightnings,
and an imago burst out having wings
and old chant of a locust.
The silenced hosannahs might sound again in solitudes,
one pair of snow leopards survive on a broken-off crest.
A few wolves too might miraculously live on,
though now we cannot imagine.

Ashes and death might return in forms
responsive to kindness and intelligence
as a noble horse comes to the held-out hand

of one who raised it with gentleness.
I have seen the beautiful upward leap of a deer, feet drawn together,
and the way a great heron flies with legs trailing elegantly behind.
Animals just old enough to walk
will come to a human, hungry and willingly.

Beside highways of cities weed flowers open between summer heat
    and the coming freeze—
clover, sedge, polygonum, sedums, goldenrod,
herbs and weeds blooming in the path of exhaust gases of trucks.
Ants, spiders, beetles, flies, mosquitoes, bees, worms,
live well in even the dirtiest places,
live over-abundant, not cherished, but having struggled out
into form and escape, spreading through regenerative generations.

Dying and creating, we humans did not begin them,
we resulted from them,
and the dead fish and birds we ate after slaughter,
the fields we burned and planted, crowded, destroyed, sustained us.
The simple existing of all forms
and tender nurturing,
can they be resurrected and create sensate lives again?
Turtles, cockroaches, dragonflies are forms
survived from past tumults on earth.
They remember in their genes what no person knows,
and have shared the entire existence of civilizations intimately.

Surely they must remain after all others have vanished.
But where would there still be sunlit green fields, ponds,
dark cracks and corners where they might hibernate
    or their eggs survive?
After cataclysmic fires
will there even be enough moisture remaining
for any sort of solitary tears?

Lamentation of the Rocks

Robert O'Rourke

Robert O'Rourke, is poet, wood-carver and environmental activist living in Colorado. This modern day St. Francis says: "My poem was written during a trip to the Navajo Nation with my son, David. We crossed the Chuska Mountains on a rough, rugged road before we came to a place called Canyon to Chelly. All along the route trees were bulldozed, rocks dynamited, the earth broken and scarred. It seemed to me that even the rocks cried out in pain. Wildlife must have been panicked by the blasting and desolation of their homes and habitat. It was enough to make us depressed and heart-broken."

Long ago nature's music played along
the slopes of our sacred Chuska Mountains;
their bright melodies lingered deep in the valleys.
My people, the Dineh, took solace in
wind whispers,
coyote songs,
the silence of rocks and
high-soaring eagles.
Today I return to this place where my ancestors
gathered medicine herbs.
I stop to listen for the old melodies
running softly through the trees,
for the beating heart of Mother Earth,
the rhythm of sparkling waters.
The sonorous sounds are no more!
What remain are
lamentations of blasted boulders,
clanking of chain saws,
crashing trees,
rocks crumbling into dust.

My spirit yearns for the long-ago, lost harmonies—-
    the musing of insects,
        rustle of leaves,
            the voice of the hawk.
Stooping down, I choose one tormented rock;
    holding it gently toward the sky;
        together we pray to the GOD-OF-ALL-THINGS
            for the return of earth song,
                the murmur of grass,
                    butterfly wings and
                        the gentle silence of rocks
                            at peace.

Tragic Error

Denise Levertov

Denise Levertov (1923-1997) was born in Ilford, Essex, England. Educated privately, she emigrated to the United States. in 1948. She taught in many institutions, notably at Stanford University, and is known for her poetry of political and social activism. Do you agree with her that the word from the Genesis creation story, "subdue," lies at the root of humankind's plundering of the Planet Earth?

The earth is the Lord's, we gabbled,
and the fullness thereof—
while we looted and pillaged, claiming indemnity:
the fullness thereof
given over to us, to our use—
while we preened ourselves, sure of our power,
willful or ignorant, through the centuries.

Miswritten, misread, that charge:
Subdue was the false, the misplaced word in the story.
Surely we were to have been
Earth's mind, mirror, reflective source.
Surely our task
Was to have been
To love the earth,
To dress and keep it like Eden's garden.

That would have been our dominion:
to be those cells of earth's body that could
perceive and imagine, could bring the planet
into the haven it is to be known,
(as the eye blesses the hand, perceiving
its form and the work it can do).

The Spring Forest

Geoffrey Lehmann

We have entered a period of mass extinction of species—the largest die-off in sixty-five million years. The World Conservation Union has informed us that one quarter of the world's mammals and thirteen percent of plant species are threatened with extinction. When species are lost, we lose precious links—"gaps in the text"—with the continuity of life of earth. This poem is by the contemporary Australian poet, Geoffrey Lehmann (b. 1940).

Each year we get further away
from the Spring Forest,
the original text.

'Drinking straws' we say,
sipping a milkshake of imitation vanilla
through a thin plastic tube.
My children in summer
used stubble from paddocks
for sipping crushed strawberry water.
These days you don't find tadpoles
boiling up in the washing.

Each year
there are more gaps in the text,
privet in creekbeds
chokes out she-oak,
weeds blot the lettering.

Each place spoke through its plants
and fauna, until we came.

Greetings to All Afric's Lands—East, North, South, West

Sam Epelle

Born in Ibadan, Nigeria, Sam Epelle eloquently describes an Edenic Africa, rich in flora and fauna, yet he laments the destruction caused by the machete and what we now know as "slash and burn" techniques to level the ground. When this poem was written, probably in the middle of the last century, Epelle could not have begun to imagine just how much more Africa's flourishing lands would ultimately be stripped of resources and drenched with the blood of war and civil unrest.

Greetings to lands of yams and palm;
Greetings to lands of cocoa and groundnuts;
Greetings to lands of gold;
Greetings to lands of plenty, maize and bananas and oranges;
Greetings to lands of coffee and rice;
Greetings to Sahara, Kalahari, Nile, Niger, Congo, Zambesi and all;
Greetings to mangrove swamps, sandy shores, forests;
Greetings to huts and houses, cities and villages;
Greetings to the leopard, monkey, elephant, hippo, ostrich, vulture,
  chimpanzee, crocodile;
Greetings, kind and true, to other beasts and other birds.
Afric's lands of good, brave men with souls their own,
Lands of strong men with heads raised high;
They are great lands—Afric's lands of machete.
The farm in the forest, the machete that clears the bush;
The farmer's hut, the yams stacked high in the barn already for the
  market;
The leaves of the cocoyam spreading to welcome the harvest that must
  ruin them;
The twitting of the sparrow;
The hoot of the owl;
The cooing of the pigeon;
The twig that breaks under the foot and you look around.

There is no cause for alarm; you go forward.
Farmland spreads hither and thither;
Yam tendrils coil around tall bamboo poles;
Banana and rubber plantations spread far and wide—there is no end to the cavalcade.
The cutting of the palm fruit;
The tapping of the rubber;
The struggle of men who sought to end the slave trade and bring peace to Afric's lands—
Freetown, Liberia, Wilberforce, Livingstone, the Slave Coast,
Zanzibar and Liberty;
The fight, the victory, the death, to lighten darkness;
The memories of bygone days;
The hopes of the future;
The momentary joy of actions taken by themselves, of homes which they call their own.
Machete, Cham!
The thick forest, before the onslaught,
Trees and shrubs tumble down all flat;
A big fire razes all to ashes.
Machete, Zam!
The sapling falls, the ground is cleared;
Houses rise, with raffia roofs and muddy walls;
Or the farm hoed out with care and toil
Is ready for the planting—yams and cassava; greens and pumpkins;
And so from day to day the machete rises, falls,
And time moves on in Afric's lands.

The Dream of the Earth

Lift up your eyes upon
the day breaking for you.

Give birth again
to the dream.

—Maya Angelou,
"On the Pulse of Morning"

New Heavens and a New Earth

Isaiah 65

Adapted by Anne Rowthorn

God, speaking through the Hebrew prophet, Isaiah, presents an image of a new heaven and a new earth in which all creation will be united, renewed, refreshed, and transformed. This idea finds its final restatement in the culminating chapter of the New Testament in which John has a vision of the New Jerusalem: "Then I saw a new heaven and a new earth. . . . "(Rev. 21:1).

I am about to create new heavens and a new earth. The former things shall not be remembered or come to mind. Be glad and rejoice forever in what I am creating; for I am about to create Jerusalem as a joy, and its people as a delight. I will rejoice in Jerusalem, and delight in my people; no more shall the sound of weeping be heard in it, or the cry of distress. No more shall there be in infant who lives but a few days, or an old person who does not live out a lifetime; for one who dies at a hundred years will be considered a youth, and one who falls short of a hundred will be considered accursed.

People will build houses and inhabit them; they shall plant vineyards and eat their fruit. They shall not build and another inhabit; they shall not plant and another eat; for like the days of a tree shall the days of my people be, and my chosen shall long enjoy the work of their hands.

My people shall not labor in vain, or bear children for calamity. They shall be the offspring blessed by God, and their descendants shall be blessed for all time to come.

Before they call I will answer. While they are yet speaking I will hear. The wolf and lamb shall feed together, the lion shall eat straw like the ox. They shall not hurt or destroy on all my holy mountain.

Our Deepest Fear

Nelson Mandela

"You are a child of the Universe," Nelson Mandela reminds us, and as we liberate ourselves we liberate those around us. He should know! Born in a simple village in South Africa, he spent twenty-seven years as a political prisoner before becoming that country's first black president. A fearless fighter against all injustice, Mandela's leadership accomplished the seemingly insurmountable task of dismantling apartheid.

Our deepest fear is not that we are inadequate.
Our deepest fear is that we are powerful beyond measure.
It is our light, not our darkness,
 that frightens us.
We ask ourselves,
"Who am I to be brilliant, gorgeous, talented, fabulous?"
Actually, who are you not to be?
You are a child of the Universe.
Your playing small does not serve the world.
There is nothing enlightened about shrinking so that other people
 won't feel insecure around you.
You were born to manifest he glory that is in you.
It is not just in some of us,
 it is in everyone.
And as we let our own light shine,
 we unconsciously give other people
 permission to do the same.
And as we are liberated from our own fear,
 Our presence automatically
 liberates others.

Warriors of the Rainbow

William Willoya and Vinson Brown

A copy of the book containing this message was taken by the crew of the Phyllis Cormack on the first Greenpeace campaign to Amchitka in the Aleutian Islands in September, 1971. This legend expressed the spiritual framework for Greenpeace. From it, Greenpeace took the name of the flagship of their fleet, the "Rainbow Warrior," which was tragically destroyed in an act of sabotage in Auckland, New Zealand, on July 10, 1985.

An old Indian woman told the following story to her great grandson:

In their dreams the old ones saw that the Indians would go through a very bad time, that they would lose their spirit, that they would be split up into many parts by the different kinds of religion of the white people. Like them, they would try to find what these strange people call success. But one day the Indians would begin to wake up, the old ones told me. They would see that those white people who chased after personal pleasure left behind the truly important things in life. The Indians would see that their people in the old days were in tune with something far more wonderful; they were in harmony with the Spirit of Life.

And you must realize that this is not all the old ones saw in their dreams. They saw that just when the Indians seemed to be all becoming like the more foolish white people, just when everybody thought they had forgotten about the ancient days, at that time a great light would come from the east. It would come into the hearts of some of the Indians, and they would become like the prairie fire, spreading not only love between all races, but also between the different religions.

This light you must find, O son of my son's son, my beloved, and I believe that when you seek for your vision on the mountain top you will be told how to find it. For it will be something so big and wonderful that in it all peoples of the world can find shelter. And, in that day all the little circles will come under the one big circle of understanding and unity.

As she stopped talking, the old woman and the boy looked to the east and they saw a great rainbow flaming in the sky where a thunderstorm had passed.

The rainbow is a sign from the Great Spirit who is in all things. It is a sign of the union of all people like one big family. Go to the mountain top, child of my flesh, and learn to be a Warrior of the Rainbow, for it is only by spreading love and joy to others that hate in this world can be changed to understanding and kindness, and war and destruction shall end.

The Once and Future Planet

Ellen

Ellen, a Belgian student writing in Children's State of the World Handbook, *takes a long view of life, for she has a vision of the earth finally returning to a pristine state of paradise.*

There was once a beautiful planet
With turquoise seas, emerald forests and skies of blue,
And on this planet were born living creatures.
Everything was clean and new
Until something happened.
A new creature standing on two feet appeared.
He had a new thing called intelligence.
He became a master of all the other creatures.
He began building houses to live in,
Bridges to cross rivers never crossed before.
And slowly he started wrecking the beautiful countryside
Until one day, the beautiful planet was a home no more to man.
And it returned to its beautiful old self after a while;
Peaceful, clean and beautiful,
It seemed as if man was just
A passing thing.

The Single Universe Community

Thomas Berry

One of the United States' preeminent spokespersons for the earth, Thomas Berry tells us that "The Great Work" of us all is to carry out the transition from a period of human devastation of the planet to a period when humans are present to the planet in a mutually beneficial manner. The primary guide to the future, the primary university, becomes the universe itself.

The story of the universe is now being told. . . . We begin to understand our human identity with all other modes of existence that constitute with us the single universe community. The one story includes us all. We are, everyone, cousins of one another. Every being is intimately present to and immediately influencing every other being.

We see quite clearly that what happens to the non-human happens to the human, What happens to the outer world happens to the inner world. If the outer world is diminished in its grandeur than the emotional, imaginative, intellectual, and spiritual life of the human is diminished or extinguished. Without the soaring birds, the great forests, the sounds and coloration of the insects, the free-flowing streams, the flowering fields, the sight of the clouds by day and the stars at night, we become impoverished in all that makes us human.

There is now developing a profound mystique of the natural world. Beyond the technical comprehension of what is happening and the directions in which we need to change, we now experience the deep mysteries of existence through the wonders of the world about us. . . .

We are now experiencing a moment of significance far beyond what any of us can imagine. It can be said that the foundations of a new historical period, the Ecozoic Era, have been established in every realm of human affairs. The mythic vision has been set in place. The distorted dream of an industrial technological paradise is being replaced by the more viable dream of a mutually enhancing human presence within an ever-renewing organic-based earth community. The dream drives the action. In the larger cultural context the dream becomes the myth that both guides and drives the action.

But even as we make our transition into this new century we must note that moments of grace are transient moments. The transformation must take place within a brief period. Otherwise it is gone forever. In the immense story of the universe, that so many of these moments have been navigated successfully is some indication that the universe is for us rather than against us. We only need to summon these forces to our support in order to succeed. . . .

Logos

Kristen Poirier

The students in the Ecology and Justice course I was teaching were asked to adapt a Biblical passage for contemporary use with an ecological theme. Kristin Poirier wrote this poetic meditation on John 1:1, "In the beginning was the Word, and the Word was with God. . . ."

God calls,
　　and the ebony sky sparkles
　　　　in the reflected light of the new day,
　　　　　　and then steals away silently,
　　　　　　　　trailing behind her dusky hues
　　　　　　　　　　of the breaking dawn.

God yawns,
　　and the earth awakens
　　　　in the breath of a morning glory
　　　　　　unfolding her white silken arms
　　　　　　　　to embrace the rising sun.

God sighs,
　　and the great blue heron
　　　　wings silently from his hiding place
　　　　　　leaving small rippled prints,
　　　　　　in the mirrored surface
　　　　　　　　of the sleeping lake.

God laughs,
　　and the burnished coat of the otter
　　　　gleams in the winter sun
　　　　　　as he slides merrily down
　　　　　　the snowy hillside
　　　　　　　　tracking behind him the imprint of innocence
　　　　　　　　　　and joy.

God breathes,
and the noble stallion lifts his head,
and with nostrils flared
suddenly releases his power,
and thunders across the landscape,
leaving behind a cloud of dust
and a revelation.

God searches,
and the field mouse turns his head,
scanning the horizon for unseen dangers,
ever vigilant and keen
to a world of beauty
within a life of chance.

God watches,
and the gray wolf
waits patiently behind the thicket
for a better opportunity,
and another day's meal
scurries across the meadow
into the dirt,
and safety.

God moves,
and the young, untried river
enthusiastically cuts her path
through granite,
carving landscapes
and bringing life.

God works,
and the multitude of salmon,
of one mind,
and one thought,
begin their journey
of sacrifice and salvation,
that yet one more generation
will be.

God reaches,
and the ancient pine
firm in foundation,
sketches tall into the clouds
breathing in the last rays of the setting sun
and touching the heavens
with the tips of its fingers.

God sleeps,
and the silent snow falls,
in crystalline perfection,
dancing down from the stars
to blanket the earth
with cool nourishment
and a time to rest.

God dreams,
and the world turns,
once more.

What If . . .

Anne Rowthorn

"What If . . ." written on Pentecost Sunday, 2000, is a reflection on Acts 2:4, "They were all filled with the Holy Spirit and began to talk in other languages." It was inspired by a poem of the same title by the contemporary Indonesian poet, Taufiq Ismail. What would be included in your "What If" list?

What if it were not an apple Adam ate but an avocado?
What if the earth was not round but triangular?
What if all national anthems were replaced by melodies of birds and
Beethoven?
What if the capital of the U. S. A. was Mogadishu
and the capital of Haiti Monte Carlo?
What if precisely at eleven o'clock tonight snow began to fall
on the steaming streets Manila?
What if international debt were paid off by the capital gains of Fortune
500's CEOs?
What if humans felt the pain of
the boulder crushed by the jackhammer,
green leaves suffocating on acid rain,
Arctic fish choking on PCBs,
the once good earth vomiting on chemical fertilizers?
What if cattle had to hand over their pastures to
butterflies, tall grasses and wild flowers?
What if cows were only for milk and cheese and not for steaks?
What if night followed night and the stars extinguished their lights,
if the tides stood still and the winds stopped blowing?
Suppose the first robin of spring failed to appear.
What if cars rusted in their tracks,
city streets became bicycle lanes
and oil wells overflowed with honey?

What if the world's acoustics were so good that in our own bedrooms
we could hear bombs falling on Baghdad,
the rustle of a million refugee feet,
the thunder of flood and earthquake,
the prayers of children,
the gentle voices of young people making love?
What if defense plans went on trial
and the people had to pass judgment on their case?
What if boom boxes, televisions, synthesizers and I-pods were exchanged for musical instruments and every child learned to play one?
What if shopping malls were replaced by community gardens
and supermarkets became greenhouses?
What if the powers of love, joy, mercy, justice and compassion
could abolish consumerism, racism, social status and greed?
What if Rome changed places with Mecca
and Chartres Cathedral with the Blue Mosque
and Jews and Jaines, Moslems and Buddhists, Hindus, Taoists and Sikhs, Bahais, Christians (Orthodox Catholic, Anglican, Protestant and Born Again), New Age searchers and people of goodwill everywhere
were to drop their ancient divisions and make common cause with the only great religious quest that matters—
the restoration of Mother Earth?
What if ancient wisdom and common sense were directed to:
rekindling the love affair with Planet Earth,
restoring its waters,
purifying its lands,
sweetening the air that surrounds it
and refreshing the cosmos?
What if?

The Great Turning

Christine Fry

The deep ecologist and Buddhist philosopher, Joanna Macy, coined the term, "The Great Turning," to describe the turning from our current, industrial growth and technological society to what she calls a "life-sustaining society." The contemporary writer, Christine Fry, imagines in this poem that the Great Turning has already occurred.

You've asked me to tell you of The Great Turning, of how we saved the world from disaster.
The answer is both simple and complex.
We turned.

For hundreds of years we had turned away as life on earth grew more precarious.
We turned away from the homeless men on the streets, the stench from the river, the children orphaned in Iraq, the mothers dying of AIDS in Africa.

We turned away because that is what we had been taught.
To turn away, from our pain, from the hurt in another's eyes, from the drunken father or the friend betrayed.

Always we were told, in actions louder than words, to turn away, turn away. And so we became a lonely people caught up in a world moving too quickly, too mindlessly towards its own demise.

Until it seemed as if there was no safe place to turn. No place, inside or out, that did not remind us of fear or terror, despair and loss, anger and grief.

Yet on one of those days someone did turn.

Turned to face the pain. Turned to face the stranger. Tuned to look at the smoldering world and the hatred seething in too many eyes. Turned to face himself, herself.

And then another turned. And another. And another. And as they wept, they took each other's hands.

Until whole groups of people were turning. Young and old, gay and straight. People of all colors, all nations, all religions. Turning not only to the pain and hurt but to beauty, gratitude and love, Turning to one another with forgiveness and a longing for peace in their hearts. . . .

Acknowledgments

Song of the Universe only exists because of the talented prose and poetry writers, living and dead, whose works make up the book's content. I would like to acknowledge my gratitude to all the authors of every age whose material forms the substance of this book.

In particular, I would like to thank the living authors, or their family members, and translators who generously waived or greatly reduced their fees: Barb Laski, Moyra Caldecott, Brian Turner, Catherine de Vinck, Andrea Cohen-Kiener, the family of Herrymon Maurer, Jackson Zinn-Rowthorn, the family of James K. Baxter and Paul Millar, the University of Chicago, Harvard University Press, Ken Arnold, Edward Hays, Kristen Poirier, Burton Watson, Diane Ackerman, Julia "Butterfly" Hill, Peter Gold, Thich Nhat Hanh, Bill McKibben, Robert O'Rourke, the Writers Workshop of Calcutta, India, New City Press-London, Penguin Books-UK, Jonathan Cape, Wesleyan University Press, Earth Island Journal, the World Council of Churches, and the Research Center for Translation-Chinese University of Hong Kong.

This book was researched on four continents in a variety of libraries. I am especially appreciative of the National Library of the Georges Pompidou Center in Paris, the Nelson City Library in Nelson, New Zealand, the Salem (Connecticut) Free Public Library and their hard working reference librarians. Particularly helpful was Sue McCusker, who spent hours locating often rare books. I am grateful to David Barrett of the Hartford Seminary, who located addresses of former students, and to Annette and Fu-Ning Fung, who helped in the romanization of the names of Chinese poets.

I am honored that my friend Lee Bailey wrote the foreword to this book. Lee is an immensely talented philosopher who is also an ardent environmentalist and writer. There is no one I know who so eloquently articulates an emerging ecological spirituality, and I am pleased that he has shared his insights in this book. I am extremely grateful to Ken Arnold, a poet and playwright, who not only donated a poem to this collection but is also its editor and publisher. It was Ken who saw my manuscript as two books, not one. The other is *Feast of the Universe*, which is also being published by KenArnoldBooks. Ken is every writer's dream! His suggestions on content and presentation have been spare and always constructive. This book, along with *Feast of the Universe*, are better books because of his collaboration.

I am very pleased to donate half the profits from the sale of this book to the Connecticut Chapter of the Nature Conservancy. The Connecticut Chapter was established in 1960 by Richard H. Goodwin, a botany professor at Connecticut College, a man who was ahead of his time in understanding the need to preserve natural habitats and all the plants, animals and waters they contain. Almost every day my husband, Jeffery, and I hike on the lovely woodlands Dr. Goodwin donated to the Nature Conservancy, the Burnham Brook Preserve in East Haddam, or trails in other local Nature Conservancy preserves.

I take immense pleasure in dedicating this book to the love of my life, Jeffery Rowthorn. Together we've walked the ups and downs of everyday life of family, home, and work, and we've hiked hundreds of trails on several continents. Together we've discovered lands and regions and hidden treasures both at home and abroad and learned that the best pleasures are simple pleasures and that they are right here within everybody's reach, in the beauty and sacredness of the natural world. Jeffery is, in every way, the song of my life, the person who gives my life flavor, fun, and adventure.

Finally, every effort was made to contact all copyright holders of material in *Song of the Universe*. Any omissions or mistakes will be corrected in future editions.

Permissions and Copyright Notices

1. The Creation of the Universe

"Well I'll Be." Source unknown. Reported in *Christian Spirituality* (Winter 1995). *Copyright line*: The Christian Spirituality tradition is being taught in a Master's Degree program and a Doctor of Ministry program at the University of Christian Spirituality and Naropa Institute in Oakland, California, Matthew Fox, President. 510-835-4827; e-mail, ucs@csnet.org.

"God Paints the Rainbows," Barbara Laski. Used with the permission of the author.

"As You Leave Eden Behind You." *Gates of Prayer: The New Union Prayerbook*, Chaim Stern. (New York: Central Conference of American Rabbis, 1975), pp. 656-57.

"At the Beginning." Fulani oral tradition, *Oral Poetry from Africa: An Anthology*, Jack Mapanje and Landeg White, editors. (New York: Longmans), pp. 113-14.

"Before God Created the World." "The Sikh Creation Narrative." Apji Sahib and Rag Gaur Bairagan, translators. No date, no copyright.

"Praise Belongs to God." *The Koran Interpreted*, Arthur J. Arberry, translator (New York: Macmillan Publishing Co., 1995).
Original published in 1955 by George Allen and Unwin, Ltd., Vol. I, Sura VI, p. 149; Sura XIII, p. 267; Vol. II, Sura XXXV, p. 139; Vol. I, Sura XVI, p. 287; Vol. II, Sura XXV, p. 138.
Reprinted with the permission of Simon and Schuster from *The Koran Interpreted*, A. J. Arberry, translator. Copyright 1955 by George Allen and Unwin Ltd.

"The Creation." From *God's Trombones*, by James Weldon Johnson, The Viking Press, Inc. Copyright 1927; renewed by Grace Nail Johnson. p. 17.
Used by permission of Viking Penguin, a division of Penguin Group (USA), Inc.

"Creation Story: A Retelling." From service bulletin for the *Creation Festival Liturgy*, Moyra Caldecott, Coventry Cathedral, England, October 9, 1988 pp. 11-17.

"O Creating God Who Spreads the Earth, Forgive Us and Love Us." "To Varuna," Mandala V, Song 85, a song of the *Rig Veda. In The Golden Womb of the Sun*, P. Lal, editor (Calcutta, India: Writers Workshop, 2d. ed., 1970), pp. 27-28.
Slight adaptations by Anne Rowthorn. Used by permission of P. Lal, Editor.

2. Earth, Our Mother

"Nature We See." *Guru Granth Sahib*, p. 464. Found in "The Sikh Statement on Nature," a pamphlet printed by the World Wildlife Federation International (WWF), Gland, Switzerland.

"Every Part of the Earth Is Sacred." Letter from Chief Seattle to President James Polk, 1852, in *The Power of Myth*, Joseph Campbell with Bill Moyers. (New York: Doubleday, 1988), pp. 34-35.

"Everything in Nature Bespeaks the Mother." *The Broken Wings*, in *Second Treasury of Kahlil Gibran*, Kahlil Gibran. Anthony R. Ferris, translator. (Secaucas, NJ: Citadel Press, 1962. 11th printing, 1979), pp. 92-93. First published in Arabic in 1912.

"A Land of Flowing Streams." Deuteronomy 8: 7-12, 15-16, *The Holy Bible*. Paraphrase by Anne Rowthorn.

"God of the Earth, Our Mother, Make a Wide World for Us." "Hymn to the Earth," Atharva Veda XII, *Hymns from the Vedas: Original Text and English Translation*, Abinash Chandra Bose, translator. (Bombay: Asia Publishing House, 1966). Abridged and adapted by Anne Rowthorn.

"Every Being in the Universe." Based of the thought of Lao-Tzu, the Chinese Taoist Master.
Adapted by Anne Rowthorn.

"Earth, Sister Earth." *Sister Earth: Creation Ecology and The Spirit*, Helder Camara. (Hyde Park, New York: New City Press, 1995). Copyright 1995 New City, London. Used by permission of New City Press, London.

3. Awe and Adoration

"God's World." Edna St. Vincent Millay. Public Domain.

"The Glory of the Forest Meadows is the Lily." *My First Summer in the Sierra*, John Muir. Published in 1911. Public domain.
Selection taken from: *Yosemite and the Sierra Nevada: Photographs by Ansel Adams and Selections from the Works of John Muir*. Charlotte E. Mauk, editor (Boston: Houghton Mifflin Co., 1948), p. 53.
Headnote citation: From the Preface to *My First Summer in the Sierra* (Boston: Houghton, Mifflin Co., 1911).

"I Believe a Leaf of Grass . . ." Walt Whitman. From "Song of Myself," #31 and #32. Public domain.

"More Than Resonance and Echo." *Through the Gateless Gate*, Catherine de Vinck. (Allendale, NJ: Alleluia Press, 1996).
Used with the permission of the author.

"A Quiet Temple Thick Set With Flowers." "Some Selected Lines and Stanzas," from *The Four Seasons of T'ang Poetry*, Li Po, John C. H. Wu, editor (Rutland, Vermont, and Tokyo, Japan: Charles E. Tuttle Co., 1972).

"Leisure." W.D. Davies. Public domain.

"Moments of Rising Mist." *Moments of Rising Mist*, Chinese landscape poets of the Sung Dynasty. Amitendranath Tagore, editor and translator. (New York: Grossman Publishers, 1973).

"In This World." Poems in *Essential Haiku: Versions of Basho, Buson and Issa*. Robert Hass, translator and editor (Hopewell, New Jersey: The Ecco Press, 1994), pp. 158, 179 (2 haiku), 184, 192, 196. Used by permission.

"Something Greater Than Heaven." In *Korean Poetry Today*. Jaihiun J. Kim, editor and translator. (Seoul, Korea: Hanshin Publishing Co., 1987), p. 325. Copyright 1987 by Jaihiun J. Kim.

"Brother Fire." *Sister Earth: Creation Ecology and the Spirit*, Helder Camara. (Hyde Park, NY: New City Press, 1995). Copyright 1995 New City London. Used by permission of New City Press, London.

4. The Web of Life

"The Earth Is Alive." Andrea Cohen-Kiener. Used with the permission of the author.

"Widening Our Circle of Compassion." Quoted in the *Participant's Guide*, for the course, *One God, Family, Earth: Responding to the Gifts of God's Creation* (New York: Episcopal Church Center, 1994).

"Touch the Earth." *Land of the Spotted Eagle*, Luther Standing Bear. (Boston: Houghton Mifflin, 1933), pp. 192-97.

"Our Home Is this Country." Rita Joe. Original title, "Poems."

"The Past." From *My People: A Kath Walker Collection*, Kath Walker. (Milton, Queensland: Jacaranda Press, 1970). Copyright 1970 Kath Walker.

"The Holy One Has Made All Things." "Sirach," found in "The Apocrypha," Chapter 43. Adapted from *The Oxford Annotated Bible with Apocrypha*, Herbert G. May and Bruce M. Metzger, editors.
Paraphrase by Anne Rowthorn.

"You Spread Out the Heavens." Psalm 104, *The Holy Bible*. Adapted by Anne Rowthorn.

"Heaven and Earth Abide." *The Way of the Ways: Tao*, Herrymon Maurer, translated from *Tao Te Ching*, Lao Tzu.
Extracts from chapters: 7, 8, 19, 22, 25, 29, 35, 38, 41, 57, 64, 72, 78, and 81. Copyright 1982.

5. The Solace of Nature

"My Cathedral." Henry Wadsworth Longfellow found in *The Primer Book of Major Poets*. Anita Dore, editor (Greenwich, CT: Fawcett Publications, 1970), p. 181.

"Oh Earth, Wait for Me." *Selected Poems: Pablo Neruda*, Pablo Neruda. Alastair Reid, translator. Nathaniel Tarn, editor. (Jonathan Cape, 1975), p. 127.
Used by permission of Jonathan Cape.

"Nature." *Nature: Addresses and Lectures*, Ralph Waldo Emerson. (Boston: Houghton, Mifflin and Co., 1903).
Edited and abridged for this publication by Anne Rowthorn.

"The Peace of Wild Things." *Collected Poems*, Wendell Berry. (New York: North Point Press, 1985).

"To the Aurora Borealis." Christopher Pearse Cranch. Public Domain.

"I Dwell in the Green Mountain." Li Po, "Question and answer among the mountains." In *The Penguin Book of Chinese Verse*, Robert Kotewall and Norman S. Smith, translators. (Middlesex, England: Penguin Books, Ltd, 1962), p. 14.
Translation copyright N. L. Smith and R. H. Kotewall, 1962.
Used by permission.

"Walden." From *Walden*, Henry David Thoreau. (the first edition published in Boston, 1853). Reprinted in *Masters of American Literature, vol. 1*. Henry A. Pochman and Gay W. Allen, editors (New York: Macmillan Co., 1949).

"Painter in the Woods." Christopher Pearse Cranch. Public domain.

"The Stars, the Snow, the Fire." From the essay, "Three Days," in *The Stars, the Snow, the Fire: Twenty-five Years in the Northern Wilderness*, John Haines. (St. Paul, MN: Graywolf Press, 1977, 2000), pp. 76-79.
Reprinted by permission of Graywolf Press, Saint Paul, Minnesota.

6. Air, Sky, and Stars

"The Is Sky in Me." Jackson Zinn-Rowthorn. Used with the permission of the author.

"In California." "In California: Morning, Evening, Late January," from *The Life Around Us: Selected Poems on Nature*, Denise Levertov. (New York: New Directions Books, 1997).

"Matariki is Appearing in the Sky." *Ngā Tau Rere*, David Simmons and Merimeri Penfold, editors. David Simmons, translator. (Auckland: Reed Publishing, 2003).

"High Country Weather." *Selected Poems*, James K. Baxter. (Australia and New Zealand: Oxford University Press, 1985).

"Brother Air." *Sister Earth, Creation Ecology and The Spirit*, Helder Camara. (Hyde Park, NY: New City Press, 1995). Copyright 1995 New City London.
Used by permission of New City Press, London.

"A Song of the Pleiades." In *Literature of the American Indian*, Thomas E. Sanders and Walter W. Peek, editors (New York: Glencoe Press, 1973), p. 174.

"The Song of the Stars." In *Literature of the American Indian*, Thomas E. Sanders and Walter W. Peek, editors (New York: Glencoe Press, 1973), p. 146.

"Earth's Embroidery." *Penguin Book of Hebrew Verse*. T. Carmi, editor. (Harmondsworth, Middlesex, England: Penguin Books, Ltd, 1981).
Copyright T. Carmi, 1981.
Used with permission.

7. The Sun Descends Into Night

"Night, Do you Know?" From *Man this Reef*, Gerald Knight, editor. (Majuro, Republic of the Marshall Islands: Micronitor News and Printing Company, 1982).
Copyright by Gerald Knight.

"No Ordinary Sun." Hone Tuwhare. Permission granted to reprint "No Ordinary Sun" (first published in *No Ordinary Sun*, 1964) in *Song of the Universe*.
Publishing rights are held by the Estate of Hone Tuwhare, at honetuwharepoetry@gmail.com. US rights only.

"Morning Person." Excerpt From *Struggling to Swim on Concrete*. Vassar Miller. Found in the *New Orleans Poetry Journal* and the New Orleans Poetry Journal Press.

"The Golden Womb of the Sun." "To the Unknown God" (original title),Mandala X, Song 121, a song of the *Rig Veda*. In *The Golden Womb of the Sun*, P. Lal, editor (Calcutta, India: Writers Workshop, 2d. ed. 1970), pp. 33-34. Copyright: Writers Workshop, Calcutta, India.
Last line added by Anne Rowthorn. Used with permission of P. Lal.

"Toward the Bosom of the Newly Rising Sun." In *Korean Poetry Today*. Jaihiun J. Kim, editor and translator. (Seoul, Korea: Hanshin Publishing Co., 1987), pp. 126-27. Copyright Jaihiun J. Kim, 1987.

"The White Sun Has Sunk Beyond the Hills." From *The Four Seasons of Tang Poetry*, Wang Zhihuan (in Pinyin Simplified Script in English, originally, Wang Tsu-Huan), John C. H. Wu, editor. (Rutland, Vermont, and Tokyo, Japan: Charles E. Tuttle, 1972).

"Night." William Blake. Public domain.

"There Is Still Night." From *The Embers and the Stars: A Philosophical Inquiry Into the Moral Sense of Nature. Erazim Kohák* (Chicago: University of Chicago Press, 1984), pp. ix, x, and xiii.
Used by permission of the University of Chicago Press.

8. The Rhythm of the Seasons

"From the Japanese Garden." Ken Arnold. Copyright by Ken Arnold, 2008. Used with the permission of the author.

"The Rhythm of the Earth's Seasons." *Kokinshū: A Collection of Poems Ancient and Modern*, Laura Rasplica Rodd and Mary Catherine Henkenius, editors and Translators (Princeton: Princeton University Press, 1984).
Rights reverted to the authors 10/27/95.

"Green Leaves, White Water." Poems in *Essential Haiku: Versions of Basho, Buson and Issa*. Robert Hass, editor and translator (Hopewell, New Jersey: The Ecco Press, 1994), pp. 82, 86, 104.
Selection and translation copyright 1994 by Robert Hass. Used by permission.

"Spring Song."Robert Browning. Public domain.

"New Feet Within My Garden Go." From *The Poems of Emily Dickinson*. Thomas H. Johnson, editor (Cambridge, MA: Belknap Press of Harvard University Press, 1951, 1955). Copyright 1951, 1955, 1979, 1983 by the President and Fellows of Harvard College.
Reprinted by permission of the publishers and the Trustees of Amherst College,

"We Rejoice In this Season of Spring." From *Prayers for a Planetary Pilgrim: A Personal Manual for Prayer and Ritual*, Edward Hays (Easton, KS: Forest of Peace Books, 1988), p. 22. Copyright 1989 by Edward Hays.
Used with permission of the publisher, Forest of Peace, Ave Maria Press, P. O. Box 428, Notre Dame, IN 46656, www.avemariapress.com.

"Spring." From *House of Light*, Mary Oliver. (Boston: Beacon Press, 1992).

"In My Grass Hut." From *Ryōkan: Zen Monk-Poet of Japan*. Burton Watson, translator (New York: Columbia University Press, 1977); poems #169, p. 26; #626, p. 30; and #711, p. 31.
Used by permission of Burton Watson.
Headnote citation :R. H. Blyth, quoted in William J. Higginson, *The Haiku Seasons*: Poetry of the Natural World (New York: Kodansha International, 1996), p. 26.

"Cuckoo Songs." *Ryōkan: Zen Monk-Poet of Japan*. Burton Watson, translator (New York: Columbia University Press, 1977), poems #669 and #672, p. 32.
Used by permission of Burton Watson.

"The First Fall Winds." *Ryōkan: Zen Monk-Poet of Japan*. Burton Watson, translator (New York: Columbia University Press, 1977), poems #153, p. 37; #820, p. 39; #826, p. 36; #748, p. 38.
Used by permission of Burton Watson.

"The Dark of Winter." *Ryōkan: Zen-Poet of Japan*. Burton Watson, translator (New York: Columbia University Press, 1977), poem #47, p. 85.
Used by permission of Burton Watson.

"Behold the Spring Has Come." Chief Sitting Bull. Source unknown.

"Ten Thousand Things Respond to Spring Sun." In *An Introduction to Sung Poetry*, Ed. by Kojiro Yoshikawa. Tr. by Burton Watson (Cambridge, MA: Harvard University Press, 1967).
Copyright 1976 by the Harvard-Yenching Institute.
Reprinted by permission of Harvard University Press.

"The Spring Equinox." In *Prayers for a Planetary Pilgrim: A Personal Manual for Prayer and Ritual,* Edward Hays. (Easton, KS: Forest of Peace Books, 1988), p. 19. Used with permission of the publisher, Forest of Peace, Ave Maria Press, P. O. Box 428, Notre Dame, IN 46656, www.avemariapress.com.

"Midsummer's Eve." Diane Ackerman, author. Excerpted from "Summer," in *The Nature of Nature: New Essays From America's Finest Writers on Nature,* William H. Shore, editor (New York/San Diego/London: Harcourt Brace and Co., 1994). Used by permission of Diane Ackerman, author.
Headnote citation:Diane Ackerman, Interview with Linda Richards, *January Magazine,* August, 1999.

"Nothing Gold Can Stay." From *The Poetry of Robert Frost,* Edward Connery Lathem, editor. Copyright 1942, 1951; 1962 by Robert Frost. Copyright 1970 by Lesley Frost Ballantine. Copyright 1923, 1934, 1969 by Henry Holt and Company, LLC. Reprinted by permission of Henry Holt and Company, LLC.
Headnote citation: From a letter written by Robert Frost, quoted in *Robert Frost's Poems.* Louis Untermeyer, editor (New York: Washington Square Press, 1946,1967), p.224.

"The First Snow of the Year." In *Japanese Haiku, vol. 4,* Winter, R. H. Blyth, editor (Tokyo: Hokuseido Press, 1952). Copyright 1952, 1953, translated by R. H. Blyth. Used by permission of Hokuseido Press.

"Snow Is Falling." From *In the Interlude Poems: 1945-1960.* Henry Kamen, translator (London: Oxford University Press, 1962), pp. 90-91. English translation copyright Henry Kamen, 1962.

9. Forests and Mountains

"September." From *Selected Poems 1975-2000,* Lauris Edmond. (Wellington, NZ: Bridget Williams Books, 2001). Copyright the Estate of Lauris Edmond.

"The Snowing of the Pines." Thomas Wentworth Higginson. Public domain.

"The Tree." In *Winter News, John Haines* (Middletown, CT: Wesleyan University Press, 1966).
Reprinted by permission of Wesleyan University Press.

"The Tree of Goodness." In *Korean Poetry Today.* Jaihiun J. Kim, translator and editor (Seoul, Korea: Hanshin Publishing Co., 1987).

"The Parable of the Trees." From "The Dead Sea Scrolls" in *The Penguin Book of Hebrew Verse.* T. Carmi, translator (Harmondsworth, Middlesex, England: Penguin Books, Ltd, 1981).
Used by permission of Penguin, UK.

"Hello Tree." "?" (original title), in *My People: A Kath Walker Collection,* Kath Walker. (Milton, Queensland: Jacaranda Press, 1970). Copyright 1970 Kath Walker.

"Learn From the Pine." From *The Essential Haiku.* Robert Hass, editor and translator (Hopewell, New Jersey: The Ecco Press, 1994), pp. 233 and 237. Adapted. Selection and translation copyright 1994 by Robert Hass. Used by permission.

"Do Not Chop Me—I am Yours." Ghanshyam Sailani, author. From *Hugging the Trees*, Thomas Weber, editor (New Delhi: Penguin, 1989).

"Any Fool Can Destroy Trees." From *Our National Parks*, John Muir (Boston: Houghton Mifflin Co., 1909), pp. 303-305.
Headnote citation: From the Preface to *My First Summer in the Sierra* (Boston: Houghton, Mifflin Co., 1911).

"Offering to Luna." From *Earth Island Journal*, Julia "Butterfly" Hill. Spring, 2000.

"How Much Can I Learn from a Tree." From *No Destination*, Satish Kumar. Reprinted in Kyoto Journal, #43, 2000, p. 47.

10. The Waters of Life

"The Waterfall." From *A Golden Treasury of Chinese Poetry*, Chang Chiu-Ling (now Zhang Jiuling in the pinyin system of romanization). John Turner, translator. (Hong Kong: Renditions Paperbacks, 1989), p. 29.
Reprinted by permission of the Research Center for Translation, The Chinese University of Hong Kong.

"Happy Is the Eye That Sees Rain Pouring Down From Heaven." "Invocation of Rain" (original title), Moses Gabbai, in the *Penguin Book of Hebrew Verse*. T. Carmi, editor (Harmondsworth, Middlesex, England: Penguin books, Ltd, 1981). Used by permission of Penguin, UK.
Adapted by Anne Rowthorn.

"The Sound of Rain." Yohan Chu. From *Korean Poetry Today*. Jaihiun J. Kim, editor and translator (Seoul, Korea: Hanshin Publishing Co., 1987).
Copyright Jaihiun J. Kim 1987.

"The River." Frederick George Scott. From *Canadian Poets*, John William Garvin, editor (Toronto: McLelland, Goodchild and Stewart Publishers, 1916).

"Flowing Along the Border of Heaven." Li Po. From *Along the Border of Heaven: Sung and Yüng Paintings from the C. C. Wang Family Collection* (New York: Metropolitan Museum of Art, 1983).

"Enchantments of the River." Paulo Gabriel. From the booklet "And God Saw That It Was Good . . .," Ed. by Ernesto Cardoso and Marcos Gianelli (Geneva: World Council of Churches, l989. Used by permission of the World Council of Churches.

"River Wind." From *All that Blue Can Be*, Brian Turner (Dunedin, NZ: John McIndoe Limited, 1989).
Used by permission of the author.

"Water, My Sister Water." *Sister Earth: Creation Ecology and the Spirit*, Helder Camara. (Hyde Park, New York: New City Press, 1995).Copyright 1995 New City, London.
Used by permission of New City Press, London.

"Sitting by the Sea." Copyright Jane Resture 1999; jane@janeresture.com.

11. Creatures Great and Small

"Ask the Animals." Job 12, *The Holy Bible*. Paraphrase by Anne Rowthorn.

"The Eagle." Alfred, Lord Tennyson. Public domain.

"The Great Blue Heron." From a plaque at the City Hall of Portland, Oregon. Public Domain

"Elephant." *Oral Poetry from Africa: An Anthology.* Jack Mapanje and Landeg White, editors (New York: Longmans), pp. 66-67.

"Thank You, Zebra." From *Oral Poetry from Africa: An Anthology*, Jack Mapanje and Landeg White, editors (New York: Longmans, Inc., 1983), p. 64.

"Buffalo, We Salute You." *From Oral Poetry from Africa: An Anthology*, Jack Mapauje and Landeg White, editors (New York: Longmans, 1983), pp. 65-66.

"Bees," Luo Yin (in Pinyin Simplified Script in English; originally Lo Yin). In *The Penguin book of Chinese Verse*. Robert Kotewall and Norman S. Smith, translators (Middlesex, England: Penguin books LTD, 1962), 28.
Translation copyright N. L. Smith and R. H. Kotewall, 1962.

"The Peaceful Earth." Isaiah 11, *The Holy Bible*. Paraphrase by Anne Rowthorn.

"The Animals Speak to Us." The Indian Center at Blue Cloud Abbey, Marvin. South Dakota. Public domain

12. The Song of the Universe

"Mountain Chant." Navajo oral tradition.

"Lines Written in Early Spring." William Wordsworth. Written in 1798. Public domain.

"Sound." Kijo Song. From *Korean Poetry Today*, Jaihiun J. Kim, editor and translator (Seoul, Korea: Hanshin Publishing Co., 1987), p. 308.
Copyright Jaihiun J. Kim 1987.

"Sounds Assail Me." From *My People*, Kath Walker. (Milton and Melbourne, Victoria: Jacaranda Press.)

"Silence." *Altar of the Earth: The Life, Land and Spirit of Tibe*t, (Ithaca, NY: Snow Lion Publications, 1987), p. 40. Used with permission.

13. Beauty in a Moment

"Between the Embers and the Stars." *The Embers and The Stars: A Philosophical Inquiry Into the Moral Sense of Nature*, Erazim Kohák (Chicago: University of Chicago Press, 1984), pp. 217-218 *passim*.
Used by permission of the University of Chicago Press.

"Flower in the Crannied Wall." Composed in 1869. Public domain.

"The Far Echoes of the Tides." Du Xunhe (in Pinyin Simplified Script in English; originally Tu Hsün-hê). *The Four Seasons of T'ang Poetry.* John C. H. Wu, editor (Rutland, Vermont, and Tokyo, Japan: Charles E. Tuttle Co., 1972).
Used by permission of Charles E. Tuttle Co., Inc., of Boston, Massachusetts, and Tokyo, Japan.

"Every Petal, Every Speck." Liu Kezhuang (In Pinyin Simplified Script in English; originally, Liu K'O-Chaung). From *The Penguin book of Chinese Verse.* Robert Kotewall and Norman S. Smith, translators (Middlesex, England: Penguin Books, Ltd, 1962), p. 52. Translation copyright N. L. Smith and R. H. Kotewall, 1962. Used with permission.

"In the Sixth Month." These selections are taken from the following two sources:
[1] Basho, *Haiku, vol. I,* R.H. Blyth, translator (Tokyo: Hokuseido Press, 1953), p. 120; copyright 1952, 1953. Reprinted with permission of Hokuseido Press;
[2] Basho, poems in the *Essential Haiku: Versions of Basho, Buson and Issa.* Robert Hass, editor and translator (Hopewell, New Jersey: The Ecco Press, 1994) pp. 19, 21, 26, 33 (2 haiku), 54.
Selection and translation copyright 1994 by Robert Hass.

"Soil." Richard H. Goodwin. Copyright Richard H. Goodwin.

"Looking Deeply." *Peace Is Every Step: The Paths of Mindfulness in Everyday Life,* Thich Nhat Hanh. (New York: Bantam Books, 1992), pp. 104-106. Adapted.
Used by permission of Thich Nhat Hanh.

"What A Wonderful World." William Blake. Public domain.

14. Remembrance, Regret, and Requiem

"It Should Be Visible." From *The Life Around Us: Selected Poems on Nature,* Denise Levertov (New York: New Directions Books, 1997).

"The Book of Endings." Sam Taylor. Copyright Sam Taylor.

"Time Is Running Out." "The Past," From *My People: A Kath Walker Collection,* Kath Walker (Milton, Queensland: Jacaranda Press, 1970). Copyright 1970 Kath Walker.

"Seven Days." From *A Feast of Ancestors,*J. R. Roland (Melbourne: Angus and Robertson, 1965).United Nations Environmental Programme.

"The End of Nature." *From The End of Nature,* Bill McKibben (New York: Random House, 1989), p. 48. Copyright 1989, 2006 by Bill McKibben.
Used with the permission of the author.

"We Have Forgotten Who We Are." Derived from the words of Chief Seattle. United Nations Environmental Programme.

"When the Last Leaf Falls." *Children's State of the Planet Handbook* (Hilversum: Peace Child International, 1992). Copyright 1992.
Used by permission of Peace Child International from the *Children's State of the Planet Handbook.*

"Take One Last Look."Aditi Charda. From *Rescue Mission: Planet Earth. A Children's Edition of Agenda 21.* (London: Kingfisher Books, Earth Day, 1994), p. 53.

"Death." Aleksandra Warzecka. From *Rescue Mission: Planet Earth. A Children's Edition of Agenda 21.* (London: Kingfisher Books, Earth Day, 1994), p. 11.

"A Day Comes When Dust Shall Darken the Air." From *Literature of the American Indian*, Thomas E. Sanders and Walter W. Peek, editors (New York: Glencoe Press, 1973), p. 174.

"A Requiem For What We Once Had." Edith Shiffert. In *Kyoto Journal*, #42. Copyright 1999.

"Lamentation of the Rocks." "Rock Ritual XX; Lamentation of the Rocks," Robert O'Rourke. From *Fellowship in Prayer*, David Edwards, editor.
Used with the permission of the author.
Headnote citation: Robert O'Rourke, from a letter to Anne Rowthorn, June 15, 1999.

"Tragic Error." From *The Life Around Us: Selected Poems on Nature*, Denise Levertov.(New York: New Directions Books, 1997).

"The Spring Forest." From *Spring Forest*, Geoffrey Lehmann (Melbourne: Angus and Robertson, 1992).

"Greetings to All Afric's Lands—East, North, South, West." In *A Book of African Verse*, John Freed and Clive Wake, editors (Ibadan, London, Nairobi: Heinemann, 1964, 1969).

15. The Dream of the Earth

"New Heavens and a New Earth." Isaiah 65, *The Holy Bible*. Adapted by Anne Rowthorn.

"Our Deepest Fear." In *Red Moon River*, Nelson Mandela (Boulder Colorado: Autumnal Equinox), 1998.

"Warriors of the Rainbow." From *Warriors of the Rainbow: Strange and Prophetic Dreams of the Indian Peoples*, William Willoya and Vinson Brown (Happy Camp, California: Naturegraph Publishers, Inc., 1962, 1992), p. 15.

"The Once and Future Planet." Ellen. From *Children's State of the Planet Handbook* (Hilversum, Netherlands: Peace Child International, 1992).
Quoted by permission of Peace Child International.

"The Single Universe Community." From *The Great Work: Our Way Into the Future*, Thomas Berry. (New York: Bell Tower, 1999), pp. 200-201.

"Logos." Kristin Poirier. Used with the permission of the author.

"What If . . ." Anne Rowthorn. Copyright 2000.

"The Great Turning." Christine Fry. Copyright 2004.

Printed in the United States
147815LV00005B/110/P

9 780979 963483